Teaching for Decision

Richard L. Dresselhaus

Gospel Publishing House
Springfield, Missouri

02–0620

©1989 by Gospel Publishing House, Springfield, Missouri 65802–1894. All rights reserved. No part of this book may be reproduced, stored in a retrieval system, or transmitted in any form or by any means—electronic, mechanical, photocopy, recording, or otherwise—without prior written permission of the copyright owner, except brief quotations used in connection with reviews in magazines or newspapers.

Library of Congress Catalog Card Number 89–80210
International Standard Book Number 0–88243–620–1
Printed in the United States of America

Contents

Foreword   5
1. Focus on Evangelism   7
2. Language That Speaks   19
3. Words That Need Defining   31
4. Focus on the Teacher   43
5. The Age of Accountability   55
6. Decisive Lesson Aims   67
7. Controlling Classroom Atmosphere   79
8. Making the Invitation   89
9. Reinforcing the Decision   105
10. Beyond the Classroom   117
Bibliography   125

Foreword

During the 1990s the Assemblies of God will be focusing on evangelism, one of the three reasons-for-being expressed by our founding fathers. Ministry to the Lord and ministry to the saints are the other two.

The scope of evangelism can be described as the joyous witness of God's children to His redeeming love, urging all to repent and be reconciled to God and each other. This is accomplished through faith in Jesus Christ who lived, died, and was raised from the dead.

When the living God indwells a person, He utterly transforms him or her. Being made new and empowered by the Holy Spirit, the believer is incorporated as a disciple into the body of Christ for worship, fellowship, nurture, and involvement in Christ's mission in today's world. Thus, it is not only permissible for a Sunday school teacher to spread the good news, it is his or her duty to do so.

From this position of truth and confidence in the power of the gospel, Richard Dresselhaus has written *Teaching for Decision*. The author's rich background as a pastor and teacher are reflected in this practical study of evangelism at the various age-levels of the Sunday school.

Thousands of Assemblies of God Sunday school teachers will be challenged as this book helps them focus on their ministry and kindle a flame of devotion to a splendid cause.

It is vital that Sunday school teachers understand and use their influence to reach the next generation. Children today are facing temptations never encountered by older generations.

Only the cooperative influence of the home and church can meet their needs. In many cases the home is left out, leaving only the church to make an impact.

Some say, "I don't believe in influencing children to make choices and decisions in matters of religion."

Why not? The schools will. The newspapers will. The comics will. The movies will. TV will. Their companions will. We influence children's choices and decisions about everything else. Why not influence them for Christ and the church?

One adolescent penned these words:

Dear Heavenly Father,
May I come into Thy presence?
I am pouting and defiant,
And hot tears prick my lids,
And forces I do not understand war within me.
I need a Rock: a Standing Place
From which to face the world:
Everyone says it is You.

—*Unknown*

These lines express the feelings of many floundering young people. They need a guiding hand. Sunday school teachers can experience the personal joy and satisfaction of helping someone find the way to life.

In the hands of potential Sunday school teachers, this book will prove to be a strong recruiting instrument, furthering our goals for the Decade of Harvest.

November 1988   CHARLES W. DENTON
                      Spiritual Life/Evangelism Coordinator
                      Assemblies of God

1
Focus on Evangelism

Someone asked the pastor of a large church, "How do you build a big church?" His response was, "One person at a time."

That simple reply sets the tone and direction for this book. Why? Because it puts you at the very center—a called and anointed teacher leading a student to Christ and then enfolding him into the life of the local church. That is what evangelism is all about. You are the key!

It should not surprise you, therefore, that these pages have been written with you in mind. Three underlying goals of this book are to help you grasp the exciting dimensions of the challenge, to equip you to present the message with greater clarity, and to challenge you to sound the call with a greater sense of urgency.

Historical Context

You are not alone. Our entire Fellowship has a solid commitment to evangelize the world. Together we have marked this as the highest priority. One by one, people must be won.

When our first leaders gathered in Hot Springs, Arkansas in 1914, the task of world evangelization became the catalyst and focus for the new Movement. Sensing the brevity of time and the urgency of reaching the nations for Christ, mighty men of God established the doctrinal and organizational framework whereby that mission might find expression. From then to now, that supreme sense of purpose has not diminished. Assemblies of God missionaries, in concert with the national church, give direction to this worldwide evangelistic thrust.

In 1968, at the Council on Evangelism, this original sense of purpose was reaffirmed and sharpened. As the third point of a triad comprised of ministry to the Lord, ministry to the saints, and ministry to the world, evangelism was again given renewed emphasis.

In the decades that followed, the Assemblies of God became one of the fastest-growing churches in modern times. At national conventions, in district council meetings, in sectional fellowship gatherings, and in local churches, the supreme mission was constantly reaffirmed. It was built into the spiritual fiber of our hearts. In August 1987, the General Presbytery adopted a report calling for the implementation of a strategy for total church evangelism. Never before had the leadership of our Fellowship taken such a courageous and visionary position on the priority of world evangelization.

The report outlined the following three goals in regard to evangelism:

1. The total church must be involved in the task of evangelization: "There is a need for a clarion call to every entity, organization, group, and person to focus on evangelism."

2. The church must have an ongoing concentration on evangelism: "The vitality and growth of the church of Jesus Christ is directly related to its commitment and participation in the winning of the lost."

3. The church must develop a strategy for evangelism: "As strategy is formed, it will project what we are willing to believe God to help us do in building His Kingdom, and specifically, in reaching the world with the gospel of Jesus Christ."

The Committee on Total Church Evangelism took a final step, recommending specific goals for the last decade of the 20th century: (1) To enlist 1 million prayer partners, (2) to reach and win 5 million persons for Christ, (3) to train and disciple 20,000 persons for ministry, and (4) to establish 5,000 new churches. While these goals apply to America, similar goals would set the pace for the church worldwide. Indeed, it would become a "Decade of Harvest."

Fundamental to the strategy was the call for a deep move of the Holy Spirit. "The major impetus for total church evangelism will grow out of a genuine Holy Ghost revival, ignited in the hearts of the leaders and the people of our churches." This recurring theme in the report is a clear indication that world evangelization is consistently viewed by our Fellowship as the sovereign work of the Holy Spirit's present enabling power.

A World in Need

We are ready now to look realistically at this world that must be reached.

Ours is a day of easy believism and shallow religiosity. A survey of the average American community reveals that most citizens claim a religious faith. But few can claim a meaningful relationship with Christ. It is to this need that the church must direct its efforts.

Evidences of need are also seen in the church itself. Dwindling attendance, teenage dropout, lifeless worship, and general indifference point to the need for a new understanding and application of a biblical plan of evangelism. Rationalism has stripped modern theology of its power and influence. The social gospel has diverted many churches from a true proclamation of Christ's saving power to a secondary emphasis of social reform. The church must reassess its priorities and refocus its direction if the lost are to be saved and the body of Christ built up.

Christian educators, through the local Sunday school, are key people in formulating a program that will meet this need. To do so, the message must be clearly understood, a plan of implementation formulated, a vital concern felt, and all efforts directed toward the evangelization of the lost.

William J. Martin speaks of the close relationship between Christian education and the task of world evangelization.

There is no dichotomy of evangelism and Christian education. We will never train and motivate disciples to go into the world and make other disciples unless we inform them of their mission. We must teach converts to study to show themselves approved and to prepare to make a defense for the gospel.[1]

The Two Sides of Evangelism

Evangelism, then, involves more than isolated spiritual experiences. It strikes a balance between birth and growth. It lays equal stress on winning the lost and enfolding those won into the life of the church.

Some churches have placed a great deal of emphasis upon first-time conversions but have not followed through with a well-balanced program of instruction that produces discipleship. Other churches have been satisfied with an educational approach that seldom compels choice and decision. We must strike a balance between winning the lost and discipling those who have been won.

The dimensional aspects of evangelism are clearly seen in the Great Commission. Here Jesus provides the directive for the outreach of the gospel in every generation. If the opening word of the Commission is seen in a temporal relationship, which Greek syntax will allow, the opening part of Jesus' statement could be translated, "Having gone into all the world." This places a responsibility on every Christian to fulfill the Commission in his own world of influence.

Second, Jesus said, "Preach (proclaim) the gospel (good news) to every creature." This statement enlarges the outreach of the church to include the whole world, and emphasizes the need for a direct articulation and verbalization of the gospel. Then, in Matthew 28:19,20, Jesus brings a full balance by instructing the disciples to follow up the proclamation of the gospel with sound teaching that will produce true believers "teaching them to obey everything I have commanded you" (NIV).

The church today dare do no less. The gospel must first be preached so sinners will repent and confess Christ as Savior.

Then God's commandments must be taught to bring each convert to a place of spiritual maturity. This is a two-pronged emphasis that the church must ever strive to maintain.

A Look in the Mirror

How effectively are you obeying the Great Commission through your work in the classroom? Is the lesson you present calling for a specific response and decision? Is the plan of salvation being presented in such a way your students feel constrained to embrace its offer? What are you doing to instruct each new convert in the ways of Christ that will lead him to spiritual maturity? Could it be that recent dropouts are evidence of a failure to fulfill this part of the Great Commission?

The Challenge of Winning Children

If you teach children, a marvelous door of opportunity has been opened to you. For too long the church has failed to see the great potential of reaching children for Christ and training them early in the ways of righteousness. Sincere Christians have looked upon children as unprepared to understand the Scriptures and unable to respond to God's Word. Poor teaching methods and low commitment have nullified great opportunities for evangelism.

Over the years many questions have surfaced about the ways in which children come to Christ:

1. *When should we begin to teach children about the need for personal salvation?*

Recently there has been renewed interest in teaching nursery children and preschoolers the Word of God. For those who argue that the Bible is an "adult book" this may seem to be a waste of time and effort. Yet experience is showing that at an early age children possess the ability to gain an elementary, but accurate, understanding of God and His love for sinful men. Christian educators are suggesting that highly skilled and capable teachers be chosen for the lower age-levels to develop this potential.

Psychologists state that information input and knowledge retention are potentially the greatest during early childhood. The child's mind is uncluttered and open. What a golden opportunity to teach that child about God! In later years, bias and prejudice filter information and make it difficult for some to receive the gospel. While more formal instruction usually is not begun until children are about 2, nursery workers have successfully begun much earlier to impart basic spiritual truths through special activities.

2. *When should we ask a child to make a personal decision to accept Christ?*

Every child has a different rate of development—physically, mentally, and spiritually. It is difficult and ill-advised to seek a chronological norm into which every child must fit. Some children are well able to make a meaningful and enduring commitment to Christ by age 5. Others need additional time for development and maturity.

Background plays a big role as well. Children who have grown up in a Christian home often are better able to comprehend the plan of salvation because of family devotions and regular Bible instruction in the home.

However, the Holy Spirit's ways are not the ways of men. Many testify of true conversion experiences at a very early age, even without having been carefully taught. While these instances may be exceptional, we must accept the Spirit's sovereign work.

3. *Why do some children respond more than once to a call for salvation?*

Children's workers face this question often as they observe children making repeat trips to the altar. Marjorie Soderholm suggests several reasons for a child's confusion.

1. He does not understand the terminology he hears.
2. He is frightened into a decision.
3. He does not understand what sin is; therefore, he really sees no need for a Savior.
4. He does not realize that he needs to make his decision to accept Christ as His Savior only once.
5. He may at the time he goes forward, so to speak, feel guilty of one particular "naughty thing" he has done.
6. He goes for a reward.
7. He follows the crowd.
8. He makes his decision on the basis of a story.
9. He wants to please his teacher.
10. He gets tired sitting.
11. He responds to emotion-packed stories.
12. He had no one to teach him after he did accept Christ.[2]

While much of what is suggested here will be discussed later in detail, it is adequate now to observe that children's lack of comprehension, and hence peculiar behavior, is often a reflection of inadequate instruction. Perhaps adults, rather than children, are to blame for immature behavior in this regard.

To win a child is to preserve a whole life. It is to use the greatest opportunity there is to build the kingdom of God. And children are everywhere—in broken-down tenement houses, in government housing projects, in upper-class residential areas, on farms, on the playgrounds, and wherever there are people. And many wait to be reached by love, understanding, and compassion.

The Challenge of Winning Youth

Revolution and change are often spearheaded by young people. Theirs is a world of change, restlessness, discovery, desire, inquiry, and suspicion. Those who work with young people must comprehend this world and its problems. It is where young people live, and it is where they must be found and won to Christ.

Tragically, it is at this point the church has failed. Teenagers are especially vulnerable to worldly influences and are easily distracted from the ways of God, but the church must rise to this challenge. The gospel is strong enough to preserve our youth. They can be won to Christ, taught the Scriptures, and led into a life of usefulness and service.

The following statements characterize and describe the challenge to win young people to Christ:

1. Youth are especially sensitive to adults' hypocrisy. Those who work with youth must come across as openly honest and forthright.

2. Youth are analytical and ask for reasons. Novice teachers are often amazed at the ability of young people to think through a problem in a logical way.

3. Youth are looking for authority. In recent years many young people have found an authority in the Scriptures. In one western city up to 2000 young people come regularly to hear the Bible being taught. They find here a world of authority that satisfies their desire.

4. Youth have a strong desire to experience reality. Existential philosophies have excited modern youth to be experientially minded. They want to feel, to sense, to know.

5. Youth are highly emotional. Because of this, they often feel insecure and unsure of life. At these times they still need to lean on those who are older, yet they find it distasteful. Ups and downs are a part of life.

6. Youth are vulnerable to peer pressure. To be accepted and liked by others is of central importance. Yet, paradoxically, young people are looking for a strong and definite challenge. Many have accepted the call to discipleship.

What a challenge for the church! In the midst of revolution and change, uncertainty and restlessness, the gospel speaks of One who is changeless and who holds all things in His hands. When this message is presented in love, it will bring a harvest of many young hearts.

The Challenge of Winning Adults

Repeatedly adult workers have been reminded of the statistical improbability of adult conversions. Sometimes, therefore, the church has resigned itself to an evangelistic outreach that is limited to children and youth. Such an approach discounts the power of the gospel. Adults too will be won to Christ if the church will reach out in faith!

Listed below are some characteristics of adults and how these influence outreach to them.

1. Adults are security conscious. They are less likely to make changes that involve risk. An adult, therefore, may be more resistant to a message that speaks of leaving all and following Christ.

2. Adults are contemplative and reflective. Thus, they are not likely to act on impulse and emotion. While he may be deeply moved, an adult may not allow this to be apparent to others. "I'll think about it" is a typical adult response. In our approach to winning adults, this quality must be utilized. Christianity becomes appealing to adults when it is presented logically and reasonably. The church must give the adults of its community something worthy of thought and study—the Living Word.

3. Adults appreciate and need fellowship. An aggressive church will provide opportunities for adults to share socially as well as spiritually. Many adults have been won to Christ as they have been drawn by the warmth of other adults who have received them in love.

4. Older adults may seek spiritual help as physical weakness speaks to them of eternity's approach. The church must be alert to point them to Christ. Rest home ministry should be a part of the church's evangelistic outreach.

On every side the church is faced with exciting opportunities to win adults to Christ and bring them into spiritual maturity. The church must refocus its energies to provide a strong evangelistic outreach to adults.

The Challenge of Sunday School Structure

The Sunday school provides the organizational structure necessary to assure effective evangelism. Robert E. Coleman uses the following eight terms to describe Christ's method of evangelizing the world:

1. *Selection*—Jesus called 12 men to follow Him. This reveals the heart of His strategy—a small, intimate group with which He could personally work.

2. *Association*—Jesus not only called these men, He associated with them. The essence of His training program was just letting His disciples follow Him.

3. *Consecration*—Jesus expected and required absolute obedience. The disciples were consecrated to following the directives of their Master.

4. *Impartation*—Jesus gave His very Spirit to His disciples. Having thus received, they would possess and know the love of God for a lost world.

5. *Demonstration*—Jesus taught not by precept alone but more often by demonstration. His disciples knew because they saw.

6. *Delegation*—Jesus assigned work to the disciples. Since the time would soon come when they would have to carry on alone, Jesus patiently and gradually shifted the responsibility of the Kingdom to them.

7. *Supervision*—Jesus not only assigned a work load, but He supervised the assignment to make sure it was carried out successfully. When the disciples came back asking, "Why couldn't we?" Jesus was there with an answer.

8. *Reproduction*—Jesus expected His disciples to bear fruit for the Kingdom. In this way the Master's ministry would be widely expanded.[3]

The application of the method is obvious: The Sunday school provides a dedicated teacher, a small group of students, a relationship of close association, a directed obedience, a spiritual impartation, a challenge by demonstration, a mission by delegation, a program of supervision, and the reproduction of spiritual fruit.

It is fitting that those who are interested in winning souls to Christ should see the challenge of evangelism through the Sunday school. Throughout this study we will discuss ways whereby this burden may be more fully realized and discharged.

Summary

A study of this nature has an urgency because of the brevity of time. The prophetic picture is nearing completion. The coming of the Lord is at hand. The Church must get on with all diligence to accomplish its primary objective: the evangelization of the world. Every church must seek for new and better means whereby it can fulfill this mission while there is time. Every Sunday school worker must sense a new excitement and thrill at his opportunity to reach the lost through effective teaching. Every church leader must use all the means at his disposal to assure that the work of evangelism will go forward on every front.

NOTES

[1] William J. Martin, *The Church in Mission* (Springfield, Mo.: Gospel Publishing House, 1986), 28.

[2] Marjorie Soderholm, *Explaining Salvation to Children* (Minneapolis, Minn.: Free Church Publications, 1962), 5–9.

[3] Robert E. Coleman, *The Master Plan of Evangelism* (Westwood, N.J.: Fleming H. Revell Company, 1963).

2
Language That Speaks

"It's a problem of communication!" And so it is. We are sure we have said something as clearly as possible, only to hear the question, "What are you trying to say?" Think back over the last day or two. How many instances can you recall when what was said was not clearly understood? Or, if understood, was not acted upon in a meaningful way?

Communication is the teacher's tool. As a draftsman must be skilled in the use of the tools of his trade, so the teacher must be skilled in the art of communication. If communication takes place, teaching has occurred. Conversely, if there has been a breakdown in the process of communication, teaching has not occurred, no matter how intense the effort. Good teaching is good communication.

Many of the frustrations that plague the typical Sunday school teacher and administrator relate directly to problems of communication. How often it has been said, "Well, I guess it was just a big misunderstanding!" In fact, most problems would be greatly diminished if someone had the courage to stop the conversation and ask pointedly, "What do you really mean?" That single technique could quell many arguments and prevent the wounds inflicted through misunderstandings.

When the teacher sets out to lead the students into a meaningful relationship with Christ, effective communication becomes most important. So often people do not know what we mean by the religious language we use. What do we mean by the term *saved,* or *backslide,* or *believe?* These words, which say a great deal to one who has grown accustomed to their use, are often meaningless to those who come from a religious background that is different from ours.

It is essential that teachers learn to communicate the gospel accurately and meaningfully to a group of students who have a variety of backgrounds and personal interests. It is the purpose of this chapter to explore the process of communication as it relates to evangelism in the Sunday school.

Communication as a Process

Richard A. Hatch defines communication as a process of "a whole series of related actions which together serve the function of getting meanings shared among people."[1] To illustrate this process Mr. Hatch speaks of a communication model, or mental picture, as outlined below:

1. Someone perceives an event . . .
2. . . . And someone reacts in a situation . . .
3. . . . To make available materials in some form . . .
4. . . . Conveying content . . .
5. . . . Of some consequence . . .

Think for a moment. Can you apply this communication model to your own experience? Can you name some event that has been a part of your recent experience? If so, can you describe how you perceived that event? Second, how did you react to it? Third, how did you express it to others? Fourth, did what you express have specific content? Last, of what consequence was the entire exchange of communication?

Let's try to fabricate a model. A junior boy (1) spots a spider on the wall, (2) begins to giggle with delight, and (3 and 4) says to his neighbor, "Look at the whopper of a spider on the wall," and (5) his neighbor says, "Wow! I'll use that one for my collection."

This, put very simply, is what happens when communication takes place. Remove any of these steps and there is a break in the communication process. For example, if the boy spots the spider, giggles with delight, but says and does nothing more, it is possible that no one else will observe the spider on the wall. Perhaps a brief look at each step will be helpful.

Someone Perceives an Event . . .

No two people ever perceive an event in exactly the same way. When you tell the story of Daniel in the lions' den, you may be sure your students will perceive the event in a variety of ways. Johnny will tell his mother that his Sunday school teacher is a fantastic storyteller. Susan will complain to her father that teacher is telling the same old stories over and over, and she is bored. Joyce will be deeply convicted about her own lack of faith in God when in the middle of a crisis. Peter is challenged to go to the library and check to see if lions ever do eat people. And so it goes. No two people ever perceive an event in the same way.

Why? Richard Hatch helps to supply the answers to our question by pointing out the three variables, or ways in which events are perceived.[2]

First, events cannot be perceived until the nervous system (the five senses) has supplied the mind with information about a given event. Obviously, this may well account for some of the variables that are found in the way the members of a group perceive an event. For example, in an adult class the plan of salvation may be unintelligible to an older person simply because he cannot hear well enough to really understand. Poor hearing may also account for a child's boredom with Bible stories.

Second, each of us has a set of meanings that we attach to the nerve impulses our mind receives. For example, the smell of smoke, the feeling of warmth, the observation of flames tell you that something is burning. Why? Because the ideas in your mind tell you that the combination of such impulses means that something is burning. Interestingly, not everyone's meanings are the same. Each of us attaches slightly different meanings to the impulses we receive. This explains why one person can listen to a lesson and find it extremely practical, while another finds it too abstract to be meaningful.

Third, the way we perceive an event depends upon our system of selection. Since it is not possible to respond to every nerve impulse, certain impulses are ignored and others are received. A robin's song is easily heard in the early morning quietness, but later in the day that song may be overridden by the other sounds of the neighborhood. In other words, the students in your class are selecting what they choose to perceive and ignoring the rest. This is why some listeners will be able to recall only the illustrations you used and seem unfamiliar with the concepts being presented.

And Reacts in a Situation . . .

Since no two people ever perceive the same event in exactly the same way, it is imperative that the teacher become skilled in predicting the variety of reactions and, having done so, present the lesson accordingly. In fact, effective teaching finds its strength at this point—the ability to predict how students will react to what is being taught and what is being experienced. Put differently, it means that the teacher should cultivate the ability to know the map of the world that is within the student's mind. Knowing that map, the effective teacher directs the learning process to achieve the desired end.

Richard Hatch states that the following three questions become central in developing the skill of predicting reactions: (1) Will he understand what I say? (2) Will he be convinced that I am right in what I say? (3) Will he be persuaded to act on what I say? These questions are answerable only by an awareness of what is going on inside the student's mind at a given moment. The Holy Spirit provides the teacher with this needed skill.

Most good teachers have learned, as the Holy Spirit has enabled them, to live inside their students. "How would I react if I heard what I plan to say in class tomorrow? Would it spark interest? Would it relate to life as I know it? Would it cause me to make meaningful changes in the way I live?" If a teacher fails to be analytical and reflective in this regard there is little hope that teaching will be effective.

A case in point is Johnny, a 16-year-old, who is in church with his parents for the traditional Christmas visit. What does your invitation to "accept Jesus Christ as your personal Savior" mean to him? Or what meaning does he attach to the statement, "This is God's Book"? Perhaps it would be necessary to seek for a starting point that is familiar to Johnny. For example, a skilled teacher may begin by speaking of the 16-year-old's basic human needs. Having secured Johnny's interest, he is then in a position to explain the gospel in a meaningful way.

Mr. Hatch suggests these four reaction patterns that help the teacher to predict student response: (1) age patterns, (2) psychological patterns, (3) cultural patterns, and (4) social patterns.

1. *Age Patterns*—Psychologists have noted that people may be expected to pass through certain stages in their lives. These are usually quite predictable. A teacher may be relatively certain that 4-year-olds will be bored by a lengthy doctrinal explanation, but quite excited by the story of Jonah and the whale. An adult class, on the other hand, may deeply appreciate a thorough explanation of the doctrine of atonement.

2. *Psychological patterns*—Subconsciously we label those around us according to certain psychological criteria. We identify one person as an extrovert, another as an introvert. We regard one as very discretionary and reflective, another as passive and unopinionated. Accordingly, we predict how each one will respond to what is said.

3. *Cultural patterns*—Cultural influence cannot be ignored in predicting how a person will react to a given event. Manner of dress, judicial concepts, marital customs, and sexual mores are all a part of cultural influence. And, within any culture, there are a number of subcultures and countercultures. For example, there are ethnic subcultures, youth subcultures, and

the drug counterculture. These influences must be considered, if effective communication is to take place.

4. *Social patterns*—Seldom does a person act and think independently of those around him. Most of us are sensitive to the influence of those with whom we associate. The conduct of young people, for example, is often determined by a strong desire to be like their peers. Even adults are more comfortable if they check with other adults before they take a strong stand on a given issue. Here, then, is another real clue in helping to predict responses.

Stop and reflect for a moment. Is it possible that you as a teacher have failed to predict accurately your students' responses to the lessons you teach? Tragically, some lessons are taught to satisfy the teacher instead of promoting change in the students' life patterns. Put yourself where your students are—and teach accordingly.

To Make Available Materials in Some Form . . .

Having considered the implications of the perceiving and reacting processes, it is now necessary for us to look at the form communication takes—namely, the message. How can the message be presented to produce the greatest response? The effective teacher will be concerned about (1) the content of the message and (2) how it may be stated to stimulate the greatest response.

Some teachers are skilled in structuring the message, but they fail to convey that message meaningfully. An effective teacher is a strategist. Every move is planned. Flexibility and sensitivity guide the process, and there is a ready commitment to find a better way. The class presentation is never the same—there is always something new and stimulating.

It may be helpful to mention several forms the message may assume.

1. *The discussion form*—When this form of communication is used, the teacher and student share in the learning process.

Student feedback becomes a barometer to determine student reaction and to guide the teacher's presentation.

2. *The lecture form*—This is the most frequent form of communication used in the Sunday school. It allows a teacher to cover a large amount of material in a given period of time. Also, it provides the teacher with a predictable classroom environment. There is little worry about being sidetracked or cornered by student questions. However, the strengths of this method also become its weaknesses. Without student feedback the teacher is closed to helpful tips that indicate student needs and interests.

3. *The research form*—Especially in the lower grades, a great deal of communication will take place through guided research. A student is led through a series of questions, or an appropriate life situation, or a story that can be told in his own words. This method has the distinct advantage of direct student involvement in the learning process.

An effective teacher will use a variety of teaching forms. New forms will be tried to spark new interest and help to make the message more meaningful. The Word of God is the message. And the teacher's goal is to get that Word into each student's mind and heart.

It will be helpful for you to analyze the various forms of communications you have recently used in your class. Are you satisfied that your class has enjoyed adequate variety in your teaching form to assure their sustained and growing interest? Does the method you use most frequently relate meaningfully to the map of the world that is in the minds of your students? Do you know what your students are thinking or what concerns them most? Or is it possible that you are teaching for your own pleasure rather than for their growth and development?

Conveying Content . . .

It is time now to consider the symbols and labels that are used in the communication process. It is not enough just to perceive an event, or to predict the response to that event, or to select the best form by which to communicate the message. We must now be concerned with the occult symbols and labels which we use in attempting to say exactly what we mean. What is conveyed by the language we use? What meanings do our students attach to the words we use?

For example, what do your students understand when you use the word *love?* If they are young people, quite possibly their map of the world will contain meanings not intended by you at all. Or if you use the word *patriotism,* it is likely that teenagers in your class will have a different sense of meaning for that word than you have. And so it goes—words mean one thing to one person and quite something else to others.

Obviously, this dilemma should not be a cause of despair. If the teacher is alert to what is happening in the world of words, there will be a sensitivity to contemporary meanings. This is what is meant by "bridging the generation gap." An older Christian can be a most effective youth teacher when he understands what words mean among today's youth. Conversely, a young person can minister effectively to older adults when he is sensitive to the meanings they attach to the words they use.

The teacher must also be aware of the abstract nature of the many words and the variety of meanings often attached to them. Richard Hatch illustrates the progress from abstract to concrete in the following list:

objects
living things
animals
mammals
felines
cats
female cats
gray, female alley cats
this cat

Obviously, it is not until you get down to the very last term that the designation becomes absolutely clear. Abstract words are designations for categories of meaning, and as such mean different things to different people. Until you point and say "this cat," your listeners are attaching different meanings to the words you are using.

As you conclude a given lesson, you may well speak of people who are lost and need to be saved. Remember these are abstract terms, and each student will attach a different meaning to them. One student may assume that being "lost" means to be a member of another church, and to "be saved" means to withdraw from that church and join another. Others may respond with a blank, confused look. The words are being used in a sense that is totally unfamiliar.

Think back over the last few lessons you have taught. Can you list words you used that may not have been clearly understood? Try going through a printed lesson and circling all the words that may not be readily understood. Even words like *sin, forgiveness, faith,* and *love,* though familiar, are often misunderstood. You must take time to thoroughly explain these terms. To teach the Bible effectively, we must be students of words! "What will this word mean to my students?" is consistently the best question we ask.

Of Some Consequence

Every communication situation will be of some consequence. A lengthy discussion in a high school class on Christian standards, a chance meeting in the dime store when casual comments about the weather are exchanged, a message from the President of the United States, a marriage proposal, a heated political discussion—in each instance, potentially at least, something will happen as a consequence of the communication situation. Sometimes the consequences are enormous, and at other times almost too insignificant to be recognized. But in either case something will happen.

Effective communication occurs when the intended consequences of the communication situation have been attained. When a teacher speaks correctively to a group of unruly children, the value of that communication rises or falls according to the children's response. If their conduct becomes more acceptable, the teacher is happy to have gained the intended results. If their conduct remains as it was before the corrective words were spoken, that teacher will conclude that effective communication did not take place.

Richard Hatch suggests the following three goals that lead to effective communication: (1) to gain understanding—the learner must perceive; (2) to convince—the learner must deem that something is true and worthy of a change in his attitude; (3) to persuade—the learner will now want to act according to those newly formulated ideas.

Too often the teacher stops short of these goals. An adult may understand the plan of salvation; he may be convinced that his previous notions about salvation were wrong and that new attitudes must be formed. But it is not until he acts in faith and receives Christ as Savior that effective communication has taken place.

Howard Hendricks places a strong emphasis upon the importance of learning moving beyond knowledge and emotion to action. He says, "All communication has three essential components: intellect, emotion, and volition. Communicating to another individual involves (1) something I know, (2) something I feel, and (3) something I'm doing."[3]

We have already stated that the teacher as communicator is a strategist. He plans carefully in order to achieve intended results. And as he teaches, he is watching for feedback signals that will further help him in being effective. Students' comments, restlessness, smiles, frowns, and eye movements are helpful to the sensitive teacher as he seeks to lead the class toward the intended response.

Unfortunately, some teachers have assumed that if they speak the right words they will receive the right response. It is not that simple. The pitcher and glass approach to learning—a teacher pours certain facts into the head of the learner—simply is not effective. The wise teacher will pause in silence in order to encourage students to fill the uncomfortable vacuum with a meaningful question or comment. He will politely insist that teacher and learner are joined in a cooperative venture that demands mutual effort. He will keep the lines of communication open by being sensitive to student feelings and ideas. He will learn to read between the lines and pick up unarticulated student attitudes and use that information in planning for effective communication.

Summary

In our concern to win the lost through the Sunday school, we cannot ignore the principles of good communication. If we can plan more systematically, teach more skillfully, and relate more effectively, the world around us will feel the force of our witness in a greater way. Some have found reassurance after sloppy procedure and halfhearted preparation in a wrong understanding of the Holy Spirit's ministry. True, it is the Spirit who heightens, inspires, and anoints, but only when the heart is prepared and the mind is informed. Only then can this work find its complete fulfillment.

However, understanding the mechanics of good communication is hardly an end in itself. The effective teacher has learned to receive joyously the enabling ministry of the Holy Spirit. It is the Spirit who takes human skills and efforts and becomes the great plus factor in bringing about results. The Spirit assists the teacher in right perception; He aids the teacher in predicting responses accurately; He provides the necessary vocabulary to say it best; and He controls the whole process so that forceful and effective teaching occurs, resulting in transformed and redirected lives.

NOTES

[1] Irene S. Caldwell, Richard A. Hatch, and Beverly Welton, *Basics for Communication in the Church* (Anderson, Ind.: Warner Press, Inc., 1971).

[2] Some of the material in this section has been adapted from Irene S. Caldwell, Richard A. Hatch, and Beverly Welton, *Basics for Communication in the Church*.

[3] Howard Hendricks, *Teaching To Change Lives* (Portland, Oreg.: Multnomah Press, 1987), 86.

3
Words That Need Defining

Have you ever faced the question, "Why did God give us the Bible?" Or, put in a slightly different way, "Why did God reveal himself through words?" Think about that for a moment. Were there not other ways that God could have revealed himself? How about a series of pictures, or perhaps images carved in rock, or maybe a celestial city people could visit?

Obviously, God in His infinite wisdom has acted wisely in choosing this basic tool of communication—words—by which to transmit divine knowledge to mankind. Whether spoken or written, regardless of the language or culture, words transmit the love of God in Christ to man.

The challenge before the church is to get those words into the hearts and lives of people everywhere. Because the Bible's words produce faith, and because faith results in salvation, the church must focus its attention on the clear proclamation of these words. The apostle John puts the matter clearly before us. "In the beginning was the Word, and the Word was with God, and the Word was God" (John 1:1). John is speaking here of Jesus Christ as the living Word, but he must also have had in mind the spoken and written Word which is found in the Scriptures. Jesus comes alive in the hearts of people when His words are received and acted upon in faith. The written Word then becomes the living Word.

In the local Sunday school, renewed emphasis must be placed upon the simple teaching of the Bible's words. They alone will produce faith and spiritual vitality in a student's heart. But how can we best teach the Bible? How can we make its words meaningful? How can we lift the Bible from antiquity and thrust it into the mainstream of the modern student's experience? How can we teach God's Word so our words are significant and helpful?

Those of us who have spent many years in the church are very familiar with the language of that community. We feel confident when we repeat the gospel message that we have said it so well it certainly will be understood.

Unfortunately, that is not the case. Just because a teacher has explained the plan of salvation to his own satisfaction is no proof that his pupils have understood it. How tragic it is when teachers teach to fit their own theological understanding, and the stranger to the gospel remains confused, disinterested, and faithless.

In this chapter we will explore ways of gaining a better understanding of the words commonly used to proclaim the gospel and, more specifically, in leading people to a saving knowledge of Jesus Christ. The importance of using words that accurately communicate the great truths of God's Word, especially as they relate to children, is clearly expressed by Larry Richards.

> The issue in teaching children is to translate the great truths of faith into thought units that can be experienced. Because Scripture is a reality revelation, the great realities it portrays can be experienced on every level.[1]

Life Situation

Consider a rather typical conversation between a believer and a nonbeliever.

BELIEVER: Sir, are you a Christian?
NONBELIEVER: Yes, I think so.
BELIEVER: But are you saved? Have you been born again? Do you have the joy of the Lord?
NONBELIEVER: Well, when you put it that way, I don't know!
BELIEVER: Would you like to know Jesus? To have salvation? To be ready for heaven?

NONBELIEVER: I'm confused. What are you trying to say?

Go through this conversation and underscore each word or phrase that could be confusing to the typical unbeliever. Undoubtedly, the seasoned churchgoer understands perfectly what is meant. These words and phrases are as common to him as everyday language. Yet his neighbor may be totally unfamiliar with such religious language. The Holy Spirit often uses another person as an instrument by which He expresses God's saving love. And that person must be careful that what he says is clearly understood.

The Excitement of Words

To a teacher, knowing for sure that the message of Christ's love has gotten into each student's mind and heart is an unprecedented joy. Communication has taken place. The words spoken have struck their mark. The ground has been well sown, and spiritual growth has begun.

This does not happen by accident. An effective teacher has learned to use words in a proper way. He never teaches a lesson without carefully evaluating the words of the Bible text and asking repeatedly how the meaning might best be made understandable. In retrospect, a teacher is pleased only when the excitement of using good words has been sensed by the student.

Beautiful scenes can be painted through the skillful use of words. The drama of an event can be recaptured through the careful choice of words. People's minds can be changed and their emotions stirred to action by the right use of words. Words are a powerful tool which, when used by a discriminating and sensitive teacher, is life-changing in its impact.

In this regard, the writer will long remember a college composition teacher who repeatedly stressed the excitement of using good words. After having read a sentence, she would stop and say, "Isn't that a beautiful sentence!" And then she waited while the force of her suggestion became a part of student experience.

As we handle the Scriptures, may we never lose the thrill of observing the beauty of the words by which God has communicated His love to us. Read again Psalm 23, or John 3:16, or Revelation 22. Who can help but get excited and thrilled by these passages! Your students will readily sense whether or not you appreciate the words of the Bible, and they will respond accordingly.

Cultural Considerations

God's revelation in the Bible was recorded in Hebrew, Aramaic, and Greek. Each biblical author represented a language and culture quite different from ours. The pagan Near East served as the cultural cradle for the Old Testament; the Greco-Roman world provided the setting for the New Testament. The more we know about these cultures the more adequately we may understand the Bible and interpret it to others.

It is providential that God chose to reveal himself to the Jewish people at a time when their culture possessed the greatest similarities to other cultures. Admittedly, the differences were real, but not so much so as to conceal the truths that God had chosen to reveal.

The importance of an historical approach to the Bible is clearly seen in the following examples. In certain parts of Liberia the culture requires that the path of a dignitary be cleared of all leaves and branches. In Matthew's account of the triumphal entry, the strewing of branches before Jesus would appear to them to have been an insult. In parts of Africa only thieves knock before they enter, while honest men call aloud. Revelation 3:20 must be explained to them with this cultural factor in clear focus. The gifted teacher will seek to explain the Bible against its own cultural background and then apply its teachings to our day.

Unfortunately, some modern critics (e.g., Bultmann and Tillich) have seen such differences between our culture and that of the Bible that they have suggested that the Bible in its original form is meaningless and irrelevant in our day. They have attempted to restructure the gospel message to be compatible with modern thought patterns and verbal forms. They have both overemphasized the problem and failed to accept the Holy Spirit's power to speak and act beyond cultural differences. However, these observations have pointed out the necessity of understanding the Bible against the background of the time in which it was written.

Of equal importance is a sensitivity to our own cultural and social variables. Think for a moment of your students. Depending upon the location of your church, it is likely that you will find a wide variety in background. Consider the following cultural and social differences and see if they are represented in your class: (1) economic differences, (2) ethnic differences, (3) intellectual differences, (4) educational differences, (5) spiritual differences, (6) domestic differences, (7) geographical differences. Obviously, many of these variables are present in your class.

Now think of some of the words that are commonly used in teaching, and evaluate their impact in light of the cultural differences cited above. When you speak of *love,* think how differently that word will sound to an unfortunate junior boy whose home is broken, whose punishment is cruelly and unjustly meted out, and whose future is bleak and hopeless. As you speak of *peace,* it may mean more money to some; to others, greater freedom; and to others eternal joy. It depends, as we have already seen, upon the personal views and experiences each student carries into these learning situations.

The Importance of Good Tools

Before listing words that need defining, it will be helpful to discuss briefly some of the basic tools that are necessary in defining and understanding Bible words. It is not necessary to be an historian or a linguist to understand the Bible. Providentially God has given us various tools which, when properly used, open the Scriptures in a new way. These tools provide the teacher with an opportunity to do original research, thus keeping the excitement and joy in teaching.

1. *Texts*—The biblical text is certainly a tool. Yet a word about translations and paraphrases may be helpful. To the extent that a comparison of translations and paraphrases sheds additional light on a given passage, they become tools for research.

Language is always changing. "God be with you" has become "Good-bye." The word *ghost* (as used in the King James translation) is now more accurately understood as *spirit*. Likewise, the word *conversation,* in its older sense, has more to do with the whole way in which we live than with just the exchange of words with those around us. Awareness of the changing nature of language has prompted many pastors and teachers to use the more modern Bible translations.

It is difficult to determine the best translation. Because the generally accepted translations are usually reliable, it may be advisable to select a basic translation (not a paraphrase), and supplement it with other renderings and amplifications. In the comparative approach of texts, the teacher will find a consensus that will be gratifying and satisfying to him. In addition, he will be exposed to the various shades of meaning a word or phrase may possess.

2. *Concordances*—A good concordance (e.g., Strong's, Young's) lists alphabetically every word found in the Bible. Each word is indexed making it possible to find the original Greek or Hebrew word from which that word is translated. The teacher can gain a more accurate picture of the original word, and then proceed to find better ways of explaining it in modern terms. This task becomes increasingly important as more new translations, amplifications, and paraphrases appear.

3. *Bible dictionaries*—A Bible dictionary includes descriptive and definitive articles on many significant words in the Bible. For example, in some dictionaries it is possible to look up *Abraham* and find a full discussion of the meaning of his name, the story of his journey through life, the significance of his accom-

plishments, and his place in the unfolding story of redemption. By looking up a theological word like *redemption* one finds also its original meaning and many helpful comments about its use in the Bible.

4. *Commentaries*—A commentary comes into use when the teacher is attempting to understand the meaning of a given passage. Verse by verse, historical material, problems of text, and principles of interpretation are brought into focus by qualified Bible expositors.

In addition to these basic tools it may be helpful to have a Bible atlas, a book containing an introduction to the Old and New Testaments, a text devoted to theology and doctrine, and an outline of the main events of church history.

Words That Need Defining

It remains to list some of the words that become important in explaining salvation to students in the Sunday school. Misunderstandings and ambiguities exist at every level. Children are confused by some of the words they hear, young people attach new meanings to old words to fit their world of definitions, and even adults may not understand what is meant by words that seem familiar enough but whose deeper meanings remain hidden. Some of the words we will consider are biblical words; others are extra-biblical. That is, they are used repeatedly to speak of spiritual experience but are not found as such in the Scriptures.

1. *Saved*—Few words are so frequently used and yet so seldom understood as this one. What does it mean to be *saved?* Is there a difference between being saved, letting Jesus come into your heart, giving your heart to Jesus, or trusting in Jesus? One adult Christian woman stated that as a child she responded to every salvation invitation she heard. Why? Probably because she heard the invitation given in a slightly different way each time and was sure it therefore included her.

The verb *to save,* and its noun derivative, *salvation,* are found repeatedly in both the Old and New Testaments. The most common Hebrew word that is translated *save, saved, savest,* or *saveth* means "to deliver or liberate." In the New Testament the Greek word that is translated *save* means "to save, keep from harm, preserve, rescue."

We are dealing here with a strong biblical word. It remains, then, to determine what this word means in its original setting. In the Old Testament, Jehovah is seen as the One who brings deliverance to Israel from all of her enemies. The more personal use of the word is seen in the Psalms, where David repeatedly refers to Jehovah as the Rock and Shield of his salvation. While the nature of that salvation is not fully delineated, it seems clear that the Old Testament saints had a hope that was futuristic. They looked for a time when Jehovah would vindicate himself and establish His glory in His people.

In the New Testament the word takes on a clearer and more precise meaning. The angel announced that the Messiah's name should be Jesus because He would save His people from their sins (Matthew 1:21). Paul spoke of Jesus as the One who had come into the world to save sinners (1 Timothy 1:15). In Acts 2:21, Luke suggested a meaning which is clearly futuristic: "Everyone who calls on the name of the Lord will be saved" (NIV). John, in the Apocalypse, stated that those who are saved shall walk in the light (Revelation 21:24).

But what are we saved from? First, as has been seen above, the believer has been saved from his sin. Second, as Paul states in Romans 5:9, the believer, through Christ, will be saved from wrath. The word *save,* therefore, has a two-pronged meaning—the present pardon from sin and the future reprieve from perdition and wrath. The question, "Are you saved?" is a most biblical one. Yet it cannot be asked without some explanation. "Saved from what?" or "Didn't know I was lost!" are common responses.

The skilled teacher will check religious vocabulary to be sure the words he uses communicate accurately and meaningfully God's gift of salvation. How tragic if a student wants to accept

Christ but is so confused by the invitation that he leaves without making a decision.

2. *Conviction*—What does it mean to be under conviction? Is it related to our conscience? Must this emotion be present for a decision to accept Christ to be meaningful? Does everyone feel under conviction when the gospel is first preached? What conditions produce conviction?

The word *conviction* does not appear in the King James Version of the Bible. However, in John 8:9 the word *convicted* is found. It is a translation of a Greek word meaning "to bring to light, expose, set forth." This Greek word occurs several times in the New Testament and has an interesting variety of meanings. In Ephesians 5:11,13 the meaning cited above is clearly seen and is translated in the King James Version by the word *reprove*. The idea of *convince*, is seen in 1 Corinthians 14:24, where it is translated in the King James Version as *convinced*. Another shade of meaning is found in Matthew 18:15 which denotes the idea of *reproof*, and *correction*. In the King James translation the word is simply rendered *tell*, but with the idea of telling for the sake of reproof and correction. A similar analysis could be made using any of the modern translations.

If we bring the results of this brief word study into focus we begin to see the force and significance of the word *conviction*. Put simply, it means a recognition of error and an admission of the consequences of that error. Spiritually, it means the Holy Spirit's work in exposing sin and its consequences. Practically, it means that a person is compelled to face his life in the mirror of God's Word and either repent and receive God's grace or grow hardened in disobedience.

The Psalmist speaks of a condition of heart that could be called conviction: "My guilt has overwhelmed me like a burden too heavy to bear" (Psalm 38:4, NIV). The conviction of the Holy Spirit is an inner emotion. On the Day of Pentecost following Peter's sermon, the Scriptures state, "They were cut to the heart" (Acts 2:37, NIV). When Paul ministered to Felix, the narrative says that "Felix was afraid and said, 'That's enough for now! You may leave. When I find it convenient, I will send for you' (Acts 24:25, NIV). Whether the presence of conviction is apparent or not, the Spirit-filled teacher may expect that the Holy Spirit will help him recognize conviction in a student.

3. *Sin*—The word *sin* has lost its biblical meaning in modern times. Relativism and situational ethics have stolen the word's absolute definition as found in the Bible. Following are some of the often-asked questions about the meaning and significance of this word:

a. When is a person responsible for his sins?
b. Is sin for one person always sin for another?
c. Are some sins worse than others?
d. How much sin does it take to be lost?
e. Are there ever times when a person is not responsible for the sins he commits?

A brief look at the word *sin*, as it is used in the Bible, will be helpful. The original Hebrew verb means to "miss (a goal or way), go wrong, sin." The original Greek verb means to "transgress, sin... miss the mark." Both words have a nonreligious background, meaning to aim for a goal and miss. In the Scriptures the word means "to miss the mark of God's will— to fall short of obedience to God's Word."

The teacher needs to take great care to be sure students understand what is meant by such concepts as *sin, sinning,* or *being a sinner.* First, there must be an uncompromising attitude toward the scriptural teaching of sin and its consequences. Second, in an attitude of love that seeks to draw all men to Christ, it is essential to stress the unbeliever's lost condition and to proclaim the absolute necessity of repentance. Finally, no action or statement should seem to indicate self-righteousness, therefore insulting those who are so much in need of the gospel. How tragic it is when poor taste and offensive expressions discourage those who need Christ from coming to Him in repentance and faith. Granted, the gospel will be offensive to many, but the Christian must be careful not to be the cause of offense by his personal conduct and attitude.

4. *Conversion*—"I was converted when I was 16." "Why is it necessary for me to be converted?" "Is conversion gradual or immediate?" These remarks require a definition of this word.

The word *conversion* is found only once in the Bible, in Acts 15:3; *convert* is found twice: once in Isaiah 6:10 and once in James 5:19. *Converted* is found nine times, twice in the Old Testament and seven times in the New. *Converteth* is found once, in James 5:20, and *converting* is found once, in Psalm 19:7. *Conversion,* or related words are used frequently in the Scriptures.

Jesus illustrated the practical meaning of *conversion*. He told Nicodemus about being born again. Jesus gives new meaning to *conversion,* as it was used in the Old Testament, by depicting this initial spiritual experience as new birth. It is interesting to note how often Jesus avoided religious language and drew rather upon the present experiences of life as vehicles of communication. When Jesus spoke to the woman at the well (John 4:7–30), He may have said, "Woman, you need to be saved, converted, reconciled." Instead He spoke to her about living water that would quench for all eternity the thirst for truth. Jesus simply spoke to people where they were, with words that were meaningful and familiar, and in a spirit of love that was irresistible!

Summary

There are a host of other words that press for definition. The purpose here has not been to seek such comprehensiveness, but only to draw out key words that are easily misunderstood by students and teachers. As teachers, we must always bear in mind how important it is to define carefully the words we use so we may more effectively communicate the gospel to our world. Each teacher should be word conscious, alive to the world of words that transmit divine truth as the Holy Spirit enables.

NOTES

[1] Lawrence O. Richards, *A Theology of Children's Ministry* (Grand Rapids, Mich.: Zondervan, 1983), 122.

4
Focus on the Teacher

How did you receive the message of salvation? Was it at a Sunday evening evangelistic service? In a Sunday school class? Through the testimony of a neighbor? As you think about it, your mind will fill with the names of compassionate and loving people who served as channels through whom the grace of God flowed to you.

Even the inspired Scriptures have come to us through the instrumentality of men. Each writer has left his personal mark on his writings. John's writings reflect the meditative personality of their author. Peter's rather abrupt and courageous spirit shows through in his epistles. You cannot read the Pauline letters without meeting their author. The same can be said about Isaiah, Jeremiah, and Daniel. The Holy Spirit so directed their total life experiences that they were able to communicate His message accurately and inerrantly. But the point is this: the Holy Spirit used and uses people as His spokespersons, not only in the composition of the Bible, but in the present-day proclamation of the gospel. This is where the teacher comes in.

The preparation of the teacher, both as a person and as a member of the Sunday school staff, is of prime importance. Since a teacher teaches as much by what he is as by what he says, personality and commitment to Christ are important qualities. Words alone seldom draw people to Christ. It is the warmth, the love, and the compassion of a dedicated worker that makes the offer of salvation irresistible. Winning souls is a "begetting" experience. Souls are "born" into the Kingdom.

This requires workers who do not count the cost of love, but who labor unselfishly for the sake of others.

The Triangle

Robert G. Fulbright draws attention to the following triangle in Christian education: the learner, the teacher, and the curriculum. These, he suggests, "must be fused into one, and yet each must play its distinctive role."[1] This triangle points out the indispensable function of the teacher in the learning process. A brief summary of each point of the triangle may be helpful.

1. *The learner (student)*—Christian education, if it is to be effective, must focus squarely on the learner. He must be the object of prayer, planning, and classroom activities. The lesson must be prepared with his needs in mind, and taught in a way that will clearly relate Bible truth to his personal experience. It is student response alone that determines effective teaching. Tragically some teachers mistakenly assume that if they have covered the material in the lesson and kept some semblance of order in the classroom, the lesson has been taught successfully. Nothing could be further from the truth. The entire process of Christian education goes far afield when its thrust is not focused clearly on the learner and his needs.

2. *The teacher*—Next in order of importance is the teacher. It is the teacher who determines to a large extent the success of the teacher/learner relationship. Good facilities and appropriate curriculum are very important, but a good teacher can rise above limitations in these areas and still be effective. Jesus Christ, the master Teacher, sets the example. In a relatively short time, He discipled 12 men of limited learning to carry out the great work of the Kingdom. It is little wonder that James admonishes all those who would claim the gift of teaching: "Let not many of you become teachers, my brethren, for you know that we who teach shall be judged with greater strictness" (James 3:1, RSV).

3. *The curriculum*—Colson and Rigdon defined curriculum as follows:

A church's curriculum may be thought of as the sum of all learning experiences resulting from a curriculum plan used under church guidance and directed toward attaining a church's objective.[2]

Robert G. Fulbright suggests six questions that help to determine the adequacy of curricular materials.

a. Are they biblically sound?
b. Are they doctrinally sound?
c. Are sound educational approaches employed?
d. Are the understanding level and skill development of the learner not violated?
e. Does the curriculum plan center on the learner rather than the teacher?
f. Does the curriculum plan seek to involve the learner at all levels?[3]

More will be said later about matters of curriculum and learner profile as they relate to evangelism in the Sunday school, but the emphasis of this chapter centers in the preparation of the teacher for the task of winning students to Christ.

The Inward Journey

How can a teacher become a better person, thereby positively influencing others? Irene S. Caldwell sees the process of becoming a better person, and hence a better teacher, as a journey involving the engagement toward self-knowledge, the engagement with God, and the engagement with others.[4]

1. *Self-awareness*—How well do you know yourself? What is the extent of your knowledge? Can you objectively look at yourself? Have you learned to establish correct criteria upon which to evaluate your own attributes and qualities—whether they be negative or positive? Have you learned to know yourself without becoming introverted or morbid?

The Holy Spirit is the revealer of truth, even about ourselves. John said of Jesus that He "did not need man's testimony about man, for he knew what was in a man" (John 2:25, NIV). When self-evaluation is conducted in the context of prayer and the study of the Word, the Spirit is able to expose un-Christlike motives and attitudes. Through repentance, Christ's forgiving power is available to heal and strengthen.

Sometimes a teacher fails to communicate love because he harbors hatred in his heart. It is difficult to impart patience when there is a spirit of intolerance. Because a teacher teaches more by example than by what he says, self-evaluation, followed by self-improvement, becomes central to the task. It is right to expect, then, that a teacher, like his students, should continue to grow in Christ.

2. *The majesty of God*—The second engagement in this journey is to find meaning in the majesty and greatness of God. The teacher must lift his eyes from self and behold the richness of God's provision in Jesus Christ. Paul was able to say, "I can do everything through him who gives me strength" (Philippians 4:13, NIV).

The dedicated teacher stands in the midst of a confused world, declaring the truths of God and leading people out of the maze of darkness into eternal light. The teacher is a reconciler, a transforming force, an interpreter of God's love and grace to the lost. With a vision of God's greatness and an awareness of His nature, the teacher offers divine resources that will lift people from despair to hope and from death to life.

3. *A life for others*—The visionary journey moves from self to God, and then out to others. It has been said that if the believer wishes to serve God, he should serve his neighbor. In a real sense, this is true. Jesus said, "He who receives you receives me, and he who receives me receives the one who sent me" (Matthew 10:40, NIV). This triangular relationship is seen repeatedly in the Scriptures. It simply means that God has acted in love toward us, we must act in love to our neighbor, and in turn our neighbor's response of love rises to God on our behalf.

The Sunday school teacher is granted an unusual opportunity to be a part of this triangular flow of love. The relationship is horizontal (man to man) as well as vertical (man to God).

The teacher's life becomes a channel through which God's works may be enacted. The winning of souls is then a natural response to a divine presence that is active in the teacher's life.

Levels of Response

Why do high school students respond positively to one teacher and negatively to another, although the teachers are equally qualified? Why does one pastor have a fruitful counseling ministry while another rarely has an opportunity to help others with personal problems? Why is one teacher outwardly loved and revered, while another, who is equally gifted, is taken for granted? It may seem on the surface like a communication problem, but actually it involves the heart of the teacher—what is really on the inside, felt by others, but largely undefined and unarticulated. What are the levels of person-to-person response?

1. *The advice response*—Some teachers interpret their role in a dictatorial way. They see it as their responsibility to dispense wisdom on all matters of importance. When a student asks a question, their answer is immediate. They respond on an advice level.

For example, a high schooler might ask his teacher what he should do about his feelings of resentment toward his parents. If the teacher gives an advice-level response it could read out like this: "Your parents have done so much for you; you should quit hating them."

Very likely that is good advice, and advice is much needed. But the student will walk away from that encounter disillusioned. The teacher will have revealed insensitivity and an inability to identify person-to-person, heart-to-heart with human need.

2. *The assurance response*—Other teachers interpret their role to be supportive in nature. They recognize that the world is a cruel, hard place. They welcome the opportunity to speak an encouraging word to any who are downcast or discouraged. They come across on the assurance level.

Our same young man might approach this kind of teacher and ask what he should do about his feelings of resentment towards his parents. On this level, the teacher would probably give the boy a pat on the back and suggest that he will outgrow it, or if he doesn't perhaps his parents will. "Cheer up, things will be better!"

This appears to be helpful counsel. There is always room for an encouraging word and an optimistic spirit. Yet a response on this level reveals shallowness and unconcern that fails to face issues squarely. Our young friend will likely feel that he has gotten an adult brush-off. His problem seems unapproachable and unresolved. The teacher has come across as something less than a true friend and counselor.

3. *The understanding response*—Teachers who listen with an understanding ear will contribute to many lives. These teachers have found that people in trouble are often looking for someone to listen—to be a sounding board for their problems.

To continue with our example, our high schooler who is resentful toward his parents would be happy to find an adult who at least cares enough to listen intently. The teacher's "I think I understand" would offer reassurance to the boy who is looking for a way to express his feelings.

The understanding response level, although obviously much more acceptable than the previous ones, still does not help the boy determine the real causes of his problem nor provide him with a solution that seems viable. The teacher is rather pleased with himself for being such a patient and attentive listener, but the boy is only partially helped.

4. *The self-revealing response*—The most effective teachers are those who are willing to be transparent and disclose themselves in a person-to-person confrontation. It is here a teacher's humanity can show through in love to his students.

Our young man would be delighted to find an adult who not only gives advice, speaks words of reassurance, and is a sympathetic listener, but is able to identify totally with his problem. "I once resented my parents too. I know from experience what you are going through. I know how it feels—the despair, the hopelessness, and, worst of all, the guilt."

Such remarks would let the young man know he has found an adult with whom he can identify. He would have more than a friend; he would have a brother. Such a teacher would come across as a totally honest human being who has found the adequacy of God's grace in a personal way.

Is not this what God did in Christ? A full disclosure! God in Christ became man so He could share in all of man's experiences. This is why Jesus Christ is a good Counselor. He has gone through every experience that man is called upon to pass through. It is the marvel of the Incarnation. Similarly, the Sunday school teacher who is set on winning souls to Christ must be willing to share experiences with his students in order to demonstrate the Spirit and love of Christ.

Teaching Is a Gift

One of the enablements of the Holy Spirit listed in Romans 12 is the gift of teaching. This does not refer to inherited or acquired ability, although God is pleased to use these qualities, but to a divinely given skill to teach others the way of righteousness. The question is not so much whether someone feels he would like to be a teacher as it is whether the Holy Spirit has imparted a gift that demands fulfillment.

The Holy Spirit has given to the Church the necessary equipment to do its work in today's world. The gifts of the Holy Spirit, outlined in Romans 12, 1 Corinthians 12, and Ephesians 4, comprise a full array of spiritual helps to build the kingdom of God. Nothing is lacking to make the Church a vibrant force for righteousness in the world.

Herein lies the educational structure for the church. Believers must be taught to receive and develop the spiritual gifts (tools) the Holy Spirit has given through faith. The Christian educator becomes one who in love assists others to enter more fully into the dimension of Spirit service, using the Holy Spirit's equipment to build the church.

> Christian education is doing the Lord's work in the Lord's way, therefore being assured of the Lord's supply. We do not naturally use divine methods any more than we naturally discover God's plan of salvation. Christian education is discovering how the Spirit of God, the divine Teacher, works, and working with Him. It is allowing the Word of God to transform every area of life. It is making disciples of all nations.[5]

1. *Enlistment*—Since teaching is a gift of the Holy Spirit, does it not follow that the enlisting of teachers should be predicated on the recognition and development of spiritual gifts? Often the recruitment of workers is done on a purely natural level. "We are really pressed. Could you take a class? It won't take much of your time, and with your education the job will be simple." This is most unfortunate. Teachers should not be chosen either out of desperation or out of convenience. God has higher principles. Only He can enlist a teacher, only He can enable the chosen teacher, and only He can produce spiritual fruit through dedicated effort. We go far afield when we lift the ministry of teaching out of its proper spiritual and biblical setting and make it a vocation regulated by professional criteria alone.

2. *Enablement*—The dimensions of the teaching ministry are staggering. The following characteristics illustrate this fact:

   a. The presence of students from all economic, cultural, and ethnic levels of society.
   b. The brevity of time. The average teaching time is about 30 minutes.
   c. The wide variance in ability to comprehend.
   d. The extreme ranges in biblical and spiritual background and experience.
   e. The opposition of Satan to the work of God.

Only the power of the Holy Spirit, operating through a gift of enablement, is adequate for a challenge of this magnitude.

3. *Training*—All that has been said does not minimize the essential need for continuous teacher training. The Holy Spirit is able to anoint and use only what has been placed in the

teacher's heart and mind. John 14:26 says the Spirit will bring all things to our remembrance. When the heart and mind are filled with the Word, the Holy Spirit has a fertile field in which to work and accomplish His purpose.

The Spirit of the Teacher

How alive are you? How long has it been since you genuinely got excited about something? Is living an adventure or a bore? Are you able to share vicariously the experiences of others? When you stand before your class do your students detect a vibrant spirit that is securely plugged into life? Do you radiate the joy of Christ and the excitement that goes with discipleship?

Enthusiasm is contagious. When a job needs doing, enthusiasm is usually the ingredient that gets it done. And so it is in teaching. When a teacher has an inner excitement about life in general and the gospel of Christ in particular, student interest will build and lives will be influenced. Tragically, some teachers have neglected this important area of preparation. Their teaching lacks interest, student response is negligible, and little of consequence is achieved. Conversely, some teachers have believed God for a gift of zeal and excitement which, when grounded in the Scriptures, does much to influence student response. Aliveness! Sensitized to all the good that is on every hand! Bright! Optimistic! Zealous! It is the spirit of the teacher that opens the hearts of the listeners.

Irene Caldwell suggests a threefold definition of *spirit* or *aliveness.*

> 1. *"Spirit" involves motivation to progress toward a higher level of functioning.* The person of spirit is motivated from within to expand his relationships with more persons and at a deeper level. He has emotional abundance. That is, he is secure enough within himself that he can afford to care deeply for others.
> 2. *"Spirit" means an attitude of eager anticipation toward the future moment.* The person of spirit dares to risk. He is open-ended and ever expanding into new and wider experiences. Although he cannot know the outcome of his

efforts with others, he is strong enough to trust himself and others, that together they can make something meaningful out of any honest involvement.

3. *"Spirit" involves the ability to disclose oneself when with others.* The person of spirit is real. He does not need to pretend that he knows more than he does. He does not play a role of self-righteousness. Since his goals and purposes are upward, he can afford to be just what he is. Such is the life which fosters life in the teaching/learning relationship.[6]

Think about teachers who have had a positive influence in your life. What is the common denominator of this effectiveness? Very likely it boils down to the matter of *spirit* and *aliveness.* You were drawn to them personally—or to the spirit that emanated from them. And since that spirit was the product of divine love you were also drawn to Jesus Christ.

How can a teacher develop this quality of aliveness? One area has to do with teacher motives. Who are you a teacher? What is your inward motivation? What are the conditions which, when present, make you feel like a productive teacher and, when absent, make you feel like a failure? Listed below are some of the wrong motives that are apparent in some teachers.

1. *Teaching out of duty*—While a sense of duty is essential for the success of any teaching enterprise, it must never be a basic motive for teaching.

2. *Teaching to satisfy personal needs*—There is a certain exhilaration that comes through teaching. Often it satisfies the basic human need to feel needed and important. There is a sense of well-being that comes from helping others. And there should be! But teaching must have a higher motive. The teacher must not "feed" upon the students, nor ever feel that personal compensation is adequate motivation for continuing to teach.

3. *Teaching for reward*—Jesus spoke disparagingly about those who parade their piety before others. He concluded the rebuff with the words, "they have received their reward in full" (Matthew 6:2, NIV). If allowance is made for the present tense, it might be paraphrased, "As they are doing their act of piety,

they are also receiving their reward—that is all they will ever receive." To teach for the acclaim of others is to miss completely the scriptural motive for teaching.

What, then, is the nature of the teacher/learner relationship with respect to motive?

1. *Teaching must be seen as a relationship.* Quoting Martin Buber, Irene Caldwell speaks of the I-thou relationship, in contrast to the I-it relationship, that should exist between the teacher and the class.[7] The teacher must relate horizontally to the students. Students must never be regarded as things to be manipulated.

2. *Teaching must be seen as a partnership.* It is hardly enough for the teacher simply to relate person-to-person with the students. This, while profitable, misses the refinement of that relationship as intended by God. Teaching is a partnership. God desires that students be conformed to His will and receive the reconciling grace and love of Christ. By the Holy Spirit, these divine gifts flow through the teacher to the student.

3. *Teaching must be seen as participation.* Participatory teaching means that the teacher teaches largely through encounter and involvement. The teacher shares vicariously in the students' experiences. It is a "walking together" kind of experience—sharing the grace of God, facing problems together, accepting God's provision together, and learning to live the Christian life together.

Howard Hendricks speaks pointedly of the importance which attitude and spirit have in the development of the teacher: "The law of the teacher: If you stop growing today, you stop teaching tomorrow."[8]

Evangelism and the Teacher

Experience has shown that many people initially come to Christ because they have seen the Spirit of Christ in the one who is extending to them the invitation.

But only in its narrowest sense does evangelism mean leading a person to Christ in a point-in-time experience. In a broader sense, evangelism includes the discipling of that new convert. The teacher has been called, has received the gift to teach, and is the Lord's instrument for bringing the good news of reconciliation to the students.

Summary

If a teacher is to fulfill this challenge effectively, there must be in addition to thorough and prayerful lesson preparation, heart preparation. A veteran minister once commented that more time was necessary in preparing the heart than in preparing the sermon. How true! A lesson may be well structured, carefully articulated, and interestingly illustrated, but if the heart of the teacher is insensitive and unmoved, that lesson will miss its mark.

NOTES

[1] Robert G. Fulbright, *New Dimensions in Teaching Children* (Nashville: Broadman Press, 1971), 17.

[2] Ibid., 20.

[3] Ibid., 21.

[4] Caldwell, Hatch, and Welton, 1,6,7.

[5] Lois E. LeBar, *Focus on People in Church Education* (Old Tappan, N.J.: Fleming H. Revell Company, 1968), 21.

[6] Caldwell, Hatch, and Welton, 33.

[7] Ibid., 36.

[8] Hendricks, 13.

5
The Age of Accountability

Mary has a vivid recollection of the circumstances surrounding her conversion. She was 5 years old when it happened. A children's evangelist had just finished relating the story of Nicodemus. When the invitation to receive Christ was given, Mary felt drawn by the Holy Spirit to confess her sins and be born again. She remembers the joy she felt as she took her place at the front to testify publicly of her newfound faith. Mary has never doubted the validity of that conversion experience.

Bill is confident of his faith in Christ. As an adult leader in his church, his life is lived in clear testimony of his vibrant relationship with Christ. Yet Bill has no remembrance of a time and place when he received Christ as Savior. Having grown up in the church, he cannot remember a time when he didn't believe. And, try as he will, he has no recollection of the actual circumstances surrounding his conversion.

Most of us find ourselves somewhere along the continuum bounded by these two examples. Some of us have a very clear recollection of the year, month, day, and hour of our conversion. It is so clear that time could never erase even the minutest details of that great moment. For others, the matter of conversion as related to time and space is meaningless. There simply is no memory of such an event. Yet the reality of salvation is most apparent.

In this regard the church has entertained a great deal of discussion about the age of accountability and the ability of children at various age-levels to comprehend the plan of salvation. Parents, as well as teachers, wonder when a child under their care is ready to be approached about the personal claims of Christ. "Is she old enough to know what is meant by conviction?" Or "Do you think he is able to really comprehend the plan of salvation?"

Definition

The term *age of accountability* is not found in the Scriptures. Perhaps the closest reference is found in Romans 14:12: "So then, each of us will give an account of himself to God" (NIV). The word *account* is a translation of a Greek word used repeatedly by John to signify that Jesus is the Word, the "expression" of the Father (John 1:14). Paul points to the individuality of man's responsibility to God and suggests, at least by inference, that at some point every man is compelled to consider the claims of God upon his own life. William Hendricks comments:

> The time of accountability is the moment of grace when one is brought to a decision for or against Christ by the Spirit. This moment requires the proclamation of the Word, the drawing of the Spirit, and the yielding of the individual to God. Until this moment is possible, one may leave children in the hands of God. (As a point of emphasis he adds ...) Evidences are that we are holding very young children accountable far too much and not holding adults, who have professed Christ, accountable for enough.[1]

Scriptural Considerations

The Bible emphasizes both man's individual responsibility to God and his relationship to the community of faith. The covenantal agreement between Abraham and God, for example, extended beyond Abraham to his descendants. The same is true of the Davidic Covenant, which stressed posterity and lineage. The Jew was a part of a corporate relationship that brought to him blessings as well as responsibilities. Through the rite of circumcision at 8 days, a baby boy was formally initiated into citizenship as a full Israelite, although even before that he was accepted as a part of the family of God by virtue of his birth.[2]

Individual responsibility, quite apart from matters of birth, is clearly seen as well. Moses stood responsible before God for his decisions as Israel's leader. Abraham was justified by faith through his personal trust in the covenantal word of Jehovah. David could not escape the consequences of his sin because he stood individually guilty before God.

The subject of this chapter is illuminated by these two emphases. On the one hand, a child may receive certain blessings by virtue of his birth into a Christian family. But this does not fulfill his personal responsibility to God. There must come, at some point, a consciousness of sin and a willingness to repent and receive Christ. Those who cannot remember a time when they did not believe may rejoice that God's grace granted them the opportunity to be born into an atmosphere of faith. This, however, does not preclude the need for a personal encounter with Christ—undated but real!

Original Sin

There is some confusion about the matter of original sin. What is the spiritual condition of the newborn? Has that child inherited sin, much as he has inherited the color of his eyes? Or has he received from his parents only the inherent capacity or tendency to sin? While the questions persist, perhaps several statements of principle may serve to clarify the issue.

It is important to remember that the Bible presents man as he is—alive in the world that God has made. While one man may be strikingly different from another, they together share a common lot. The Bible makes the following observations about this mutual condition:

1. Man inevitably sins—every man has sinned and does sin.
2. Man, because he is a sinner, needs the grace of God that he might be reconciled to Him.

Our concern, then, is to this present dilemma of man. The church must accept that man is lost outside of Christ. All efforts must be directed to influence man to admit his sin and recognize that in Christ full atonement can be made. The Bible does not so much explain why a man is a sinner as state that he *is* a sinner. It is this fact that must captivate the energies of the church and direct it to evangelize the lost.

Contemporary Factors

Man's personal accountability to God is largely unrecognized in modern culture. Humanism, which arose in Europe during the 17th and 18th centuries, placed man at the center of the universe. If any god was admitted, it was the god who is within every man, certainly not the God of revelation. Man was viewed as inherently good. Sin was dismissed as relative. The Bible was seen as the product of good men, but not the product of divine inspiration. The need for the gospel was therefore nonexistent, for, according to contemporary thought, man was not lost. Such thinking is error and leads to spiritual disaster for those who fall under its influence.

The modern sciences, such as psychology, sociology, and anthropology, have historically viewed man as a complex mechanism that centers in the world of self. Great emphasis is placed upon man's survival, the satisfaction of his basic needs, and the ability of man to control his own world. The influence of such thinking leads to the dismissal of man's personal responsibility before God. Man, in this context, ignores his need for God and refuses to admit that he is a sinner, much in need of salvation.

Children, who make up a large part of our Sunday schools, are the products of such thinking. They are told repeatedly of man's developing potential through science, the basic good of mankind, and the sufficiency of human endeavor. Only through a careful teaching of the Word of God, and as the Spirit is active, will these children recognize their need and feel drawn by the Spirit to salvation.

Requirements for Salvation

Since man is accountable to God, and since every man is a

sinner, what are the biblical requirements for salvation? William Hendricks defined faith that results in salvation as follows:

> Faith includes: the depth-level giving of oneself to God—the *heart;* the full willingness to pattern one's life according to the will of God—the *hands;* and a knowledge of who God is, what he has done for us, and what he requires of us—the *head.*[3]

Mr. Hendricks then outlines the basic parts of the message of the Early Church:

> (1) Jesus came from God, the God of Israel who made heaven and earth. [Acts 2:14-36] (2) Men killed Christ. The idea is later broadened to assert that all men and man as a unit in his sinfulness is responsible for Christ's death. [Acts 3:12-26] (3) Yet, Christ's death was according to God's plan. That is, God was acting through Christ's death to bring man to himself. [Acts 4:8-12] (4) Christ is raised. God in Christ has conquered even man's last enemy, death. [Acts 5:30-32] (5) God through Christ has sent the Holy Spirit to bear witness to what God in Christ has done for man. [Acts 10:36-43][4]

To be saved a man must believe in the basic message of the Bible and, in addition, must believe that God will bring all that He has promised to pass. When this belief is accompanied by repentance for past sins, that man is then saved.

But how about children? How old must they be to comprehend in a meaningful way these basic ingredients of the gospel? Obviously, it is impossible to determine a uniform age when all children reach this point of awareness. The rate of growth and maturity varies radically, according to ability and background.

Some children have a basic comprehension of the gospel at age 4 or 5. Others may reach the age of 10 before they seem ready to grasp the message of the gospel. Regardless of the child's age, the necessary element for accepting Christ is understanding both his need for salvation and Christ's ability to save him.

Lawrence O. Richards speaks of that elementary but essential faith of a child:

> A child's simple response to Jesus may be analogous to the faith response of so many through history who have not understood the cross but who have met God in the more simple word He spoke to them, and who have believed.[5]

Questions

At this point, we will consider several questions relative to the subject of accountability.

1. *Can children understand the Bible?*

The church has greatly erred in viewing the Bible as an adult book. Even respectable Christian educators have suggested that the Scriptures are too complicated for children to understand. Babysitting has become the norm in many preschool departments and even in higher levels as well.

"What does Habakkuk mean to children?"

"How can a child understand the Trinity?"

"Of what value is Old Testament history to children?"

"Won't children be confused if introduced too early to the Bible?"

And so the questions go. By inference, they say the Bible is primarily an adult book.

However, children, like adults, have needs that can be met only by the Lord. Childhood is a time to establish good foundations—a time when the message of God's comfort and love will have special significance, even though understood on only an elementary level. It is a tragedy when the church is insensitive to the needs of small children.

The problem centers in some teachers' inability to express the Bible's truths at a level that children—even small children—can comprehend. One of the most effective ways to teach the Scriptures to children is to use directed play activities. Since children learn by playing, the experienced teacher will use this natural and normal trait as a tool for teaching the basic truths of the gospel. Even small children can be taught that God is love by guided play activity so that a certain reward of approval is given when unselfish love is demonstrated. Teachers who insist on teaching by rhetoric alone will find that children simply refuse to listen. The most gifted evangelist would fail if he attempted to hold children's attention with verbal symbols alone.

2. Can a child understand the plan of salvation and receive it as his own?

This question is more difficult to answer. It is one thing to admit that even small children can understand the basic truths of the Bible when they are properly presented, but quite another matter to reflect on the child's ability to grasp and personally accept the plan of salvation as outlined in the Scriptures.

Perhaps the church has erred in focusing attention upon "salvation words" rather than on a meaningful relationship with Jesus Christ. Marjorie Soderholm tells of a 4-year-old girl who was watching a surgical procedure on television with her parents. As the patient's heart was lifted out of the chest cavity, the child asked, "Daddy, is he giving his heart to Jesus?"[6] Obviously, this child had failed to grasp the proper meaning of the phrase, "Give your heart."

When children are told of the living Christ who will love them and be with them at school and at play, such gross misunderstanding is not so apt to happen. Perhaps a question like this may be more meaningful to children: "Will you let Jesus be your Friend?" The idea of receptivity and commitment is still present, but the language is more concrete and the child is less likely to misunderstand.

When the emphasis is placed upon the development of a relationship, a firm foundation is being laid for further Bible knowledge and experience. For example, the next question, "What kind of Friend is Jesus?" will lead to a discussion of the attributes of Jesus. "What does a Friend like Jesus expect of me?" will open the door to a challenge for right conduct.

Teachers must never forget their children look to them for guidance in determining their personal attitude toward God and His Word. Rarely can early mental pictures of God be altered. If a small child is taught that God is an angry judge, he may well retain that attitude toward God as an adult, although he has learned quite differently. If a child is taught that God is a "Santa in the sky," with a long beard and flowing locks of white hair, he will retain that mental picture long after he has discovered the original concept was wrong. For this reason, Sunday school's most skilled and highly trained workers should be directed to children's work.

Children, then, if properly taught, may at an early age enter into a personal relationship with Jesus Christ that will be very meaningful, both in childhood and in later life. The church must never underemphasize the Holy Spirit's power to produce saving faith in a child's heart. Whether the child will remember the time and place is somewhat insignificant.

3. *What is a child's position before God before he reaches a place of mental and spiritual awareness?*

Much discussion has centered on this question throughout church history. Some have insisted that a child is responsible for sin at birth, and only through the rite of baptism can that responsibility be relieved. Others have taught that children are not responsible for their sins, but that they do remain outside the church until they have gained entrance through baptism.

Although the Scriptures are not explicit on the subject, there are implications that may serve as a guide to the church. A brief survey of the Old Testament in regard to children will be helpful.

a. When a child was born into the Hebrew community of faith, that child became a full-fledged member of the community quite apart from any personal choice.

THE AGE OF ACCOUNTABILITY / 63

b. Through the religious instruction of the home a child became a knowledgeable part of the religious community.
c. Only proselytes to Judaism were asked to make a personal choice to become a part of the community.
d. A Jewish child would never be called upon to make a choice as to an identity with the community, but he could choose, at a later time, to disobey the laws of God as given to Israel and by that act of disobedience be severed from the community of faith.

What may be said of the implications of this covenantal relationship as expressed in the Old Testament? It becomes obvious that our usual understanding of the age of accountability is nonexistent in the Old Testament. Later in Judaism, age 12 became the age when a Hebrew boy assumed full responsibilities as a part of the community. However, there is no evidence to suggest that this age by itself marked a transition from not belonging to belonging.

Is it not reasonable that children who grow up in the church should quite naturally (supernaturally) come to a place of saving faith? Is it always necessary that a child be able to remember a specific time when salvation occurred?

However, with these questions in mind, it still must be stressed that saving faith is not evolutionary nor inherited. At some point, although undated in memory, the child must make a firm and personal decision for Christ. There is in God's mind a point in time when a life is redeemed.

But what about children who do not grow up having heard the gospel? Do they bear a responsibility before God that others do not? When the New Testament picture of children is brought into focus, it becomes increasingly clear that, until they reach a certain place of mental and spiritual maturity, children are in no way responsible before God—as concerns their eternal destiny. Jesus said, "Let the little children come to me, and do not hinder them, for the kingdom of heaven belongs to such as these" (Matthew 19:14, NIV). The most basic teachings of love and justice outlined in the New Testament would be violated if a child who does not possess the ability to comprehend either his lost condition or the plan of salvation in Christ were eternally lost.

The matter is brought into clear perspective by Gaines S. Dobbins:

> The child who is too young to understand the meaning and the consequences of sin, who has no sense of need of a Savior's protecting love, is too young to make the decision which will consciously put him under Christ's mastery. He is safe in his innocency until the realization of sin and its power dawns. He is saved when he voluntarily accepts Jesus and His offer of life and then, by a spiritual rebirth, becomes a child of God.[7]

4. When should a child be approached about making a personal commitment to Christ?

As we have seen earlier in this chapter, it is impossible to specify or project a certain age when children are ready to receive Christ. Levels of maturity—as well as of background and experience—vary widely. We must leave this matter to the Holy Spirit and be careful not to minimize what He can do in a child's life.

It is the responsibility of the parent and teacher to be sensitive to a child's growing awareness of a need for Christ. Periodically, as the Spirit directs, that child should be approached about a personal relationship with Christ. If the time is right, the Holy Spirit will continue to direct, and the child's response will indicate a readiness to receive Christ. However, a child should never be pushed or coerced into a spiritual experience. Many children have been permanently harmed by overzealous adults who have tried to do what only the Spirit can accomplish. In later life, these unfortunate children are confused and disillusioned; they have been told what they received without ever knowing for themselves the joy of Christ's presence.

Summary

Teachers who work effectively with children have learned to

ask leading questions and observe individual responses very carefully. When they recognize the Holy Spirit at work, they proceed with confidence to introduce that child to Christ. Since it is the prerogative of the Holy Spirit to draw people to Christ, a teacher must pray for a sensitivity to what He is doing.

NOTES

[1] William Hendricks, "The Age of Accountability," in *Children and Conversion,* ed. Clifford Ingle (Nashville: Broadman Press, 1970), 97.

[2] Roy L. Honeycutt, Jr. "The Child Within the Old Testament Community," in *Children and Conversion,* ed. Clifford Ingle (Nashville: Broadman Press, 1970), 23.

[3] Hendricks, 91.

[4] Ibid.

[5] Lawrence O. Richards, *A Theology of Children's Ministry* (Grand Rapids, Mich.: Zondervan, 1983), 375.

[6] Soderholm, 46.

[7] Gaines S. Dobbins, *Winning the Children* (Nashville: Broadway Press, 1953), 120.

6
Decisive Lesson Aims

Ed Jones is a dedicated teacher in the high school department. He spends his Saturdays gathering the historical materials for Sunday's lesson and making sure his comprehension of the text is accurate and well-supported. Ed feels convinced that his success as a teacher is directly related to his care in preparation.

He usually bypasses, however, the section of the lesson dealing with lesson aims, because he is certain that all will be well if he just teaches the Bible. But as Ed relates the Parable of the Prodigal Son, Sally wonders why the Bible doesn't say more about the prodigal's mother. Joe is thinking about how it would feel to be a runaway in a far-off country. Ruth is most interested in the reaction of the elder brother. At the lesson's conclusion, Ed prays that everyone will be helped in some way by the teaching of the Word.

Ed's approach to teaching is not uncommon. Unfortunately, some teachers fail to set specific aims for each lesson. To teach without a specific goal in mind is to let the arrows of endeavor fall far short of the mark. A teacher must plan for results by defining aims and goals—and then move toward those aims and goals in the power of the Spirit.

Paul said, "But one thing I do: Forgetting what is behind and straining toward what is ahead, I press on toward the goal to win the prize for which God has called me heavenward in Christ Jesus" (Philippians 3:13,14, NIV). The same sense of resolute purpose is seen in Isaiah: "Therefore have I set my face like flint, and I know I will not be put to shame" (Isaiah

50:7, NIV). The principle of setting specific goals is readily attested in the Scriptures.

In this chapter we will consider the importance of good lesson aims and the technique for developing them. Finally, we will deal with lesson aims as they relate to evangelism in the Sunday school.

Developing Good Lesson Aims

It is generally agreed that a good lesson aim must be *"concise* enough to be kept in focus, *specific* enough to be achieved, *personal* enough to change lives."[1] A teacher should write out that aim and keep it before him both during his preparation of the lesson and while he is teaching.

There are basically three kinds of aims: (1) knowledge aims, (2) attitude aims, and (3) conduct aims. A good lesson plan will include all three, although one may be singled out for special emphasis. People need first to *know* what God says (knowledge), then to *feel* the impact of what God has said (attitude), and then to *do* what God's Word teaches, as evidenced by changed behavior (conduct).

Ed Jones would be far more effective if he clearly stated his lesson aim. He could have selected one of the following:

1. To persuade the students that disappointment comes to a runaway.
2. To show the students that they should love and respect their parents.
3. To impress the students to repent of feelings of rebellion.
4. To ask the students to come forward as a sign of their desire for forgiveness.

These lesson aims include all three types of aims. The first is a knowledge aim. The second is an attitude aim. The third is both an attitude and a conduct aim. And the fourth is a conduct aim.

The most difficult part of lesson preparation is developing and clearly stating a lesson aim. The temptation is to make the aim too general. Once the teacher has selected an aim, the rest of his preparation will be directed toward the best method and means of achieving that goal. It is important to remember that altered conduct is the final test of good teaching.

The Educational Process

Lois E. LeBar anchors the "aim development" step in the educational process as follows:

> 1. The teacher becomes aware of student needs.
> 2. The teacher develops lesson aims to confront those needs.
> 3. The teacher structures a program to achieve those aims.
> 4. The teacher selects the necessary methodology and materials to fit that program.
> 5. The teacher organizes the materials and presents the lesson.
> 6. The teacher evaluates whether or not the aim has been achieved.
> 7. The teacher reevaluates student needs and begins the process over again.[2]

All along the continuum of lesson development the basic guideline is the lesson aim. In reflecting on successes and failures, the yardstick is the lesson aim. Most ineffective teaching is simply the result of aimlessness.

It is helpful for the teacher to ask himself repeatedly, "So what?" Or "What effect will this have upon my students?" Billy Graham once said in this regard, "If we shoot above our people, we don't prove or show anything but that we don't know how to shoot." Carefully selected lesson aims will be to the teacher what blueprints are to the builder—a guide by which to chart the course.

Lesson Aims and Evangelism

The church needs to direct itself more specifically to the task of evangelizing the lost and discipling new converts. To fulfill this twofold ministry, the church must sharpen its aim and redirect many of its activities. It is time now to consider how the Sunday school can become more effective in the work of evangelism.

Findley B. Edge comments on the centrality of an evangelism goal:

> We believe that a conversion experience—a personal experience in which the individual accepts Jesus as Savior and Lord—is the means by which an individual enters the Christian life and is the only adequate foundation and sufficient motivation for Christian growth.[3]

The sensitive teacher will recognize the essential nature of the conversion experience and will be sure that at some point during the class period students have an opportunity to receive Christ as Savior.

Go back to the story of the prodigal. The prodigal's eventual awareness of need and his decision to return to his father are parallel to the sinner's sense of need and a willingness to come to Christ. This comparison opens the door for a pointed presentation of the plan of salvation. In other words, regardless of the lesson aim a teacher chooses, it is not difficult to include a pointed evangelism goal as well. In every lesson, there will be some truth developed in a way that will clearly invite the lost to Christ.

Lesson Aims and Motives

Jean Smith is highly regarded as a junior high teacher. She is masterful as a teacher, a disciplinarian, and a friend. Her word has authority, yet with a quality of tenderness that demands the respect of her students. When Jean invites her students to make a firm and public testimony of their faith, the response is nearly always beyond expectation. But one problem persists. Sometimes the students, out of great respect for Mrs. Smith, respond to the invitation she gives more to please her and gain her approval than in answer to the Spirit's call.

Teachers must guard against student responses that are based on wrong motives. Enduring decisions simply cannot result from personal attraction or human manipulation. Wise teachers will be careful that the invitation they give points directly to Christ and focuses attention upon an individual response to the Lord.

Group pressure is also very real, especially among children and adolescents. If a student is aware that he is the only one in the class who has not publicly confessed faith in Christ, he may feel pressured to respond. Clifford V. Anderson comments:

> Many pressures operate on a child that are not pressures of the Holy Spirit. We must take care that decisions for Christ and subsequent decisions related to this are Spirit prompted and not group or person pressured.[4]

In this regard, Anderson points out the importance of providing students with an adequate understanding of the gospel to assure a firm and lasting decision. The gospel must not be abbreviated so that it is meaningless. "All you have to do is lift your hand" oversimplifies the gospel. Students must have enough knowledge of the context of the gospel to make an enduring decision. It would be unwise to tag an invitation onto the end of a lesson if the teacher has not given adequate information on the plan of personal salvation at some point in his presentation. While more will be said about this in a later chapter, it must be pointed out that the basics of the gospel must be communicated if students are to make an adequate personal decision about Christ. Clear and well-defined lesson aims will chart the course for this kind of communication.

The Aim To Evangelize

The following examples structure lesson aims around a variety of biblical passages and could result in student conversions.

THE STORY OF CREATION (Genesis 1)

Narrative—The Bible teaches that in the beginning God created the universe. In an orderly sequence of creative acts, He spoke into existence all that we have in the universe. The last

72 / TEACHING FOR DECISION

of God's acts was the creation of Adam and Eve, the parents of the human race. God looked at what He had created and said that it was good.

Possible Aims—(1) To show the greatness of God as seen in His creative acts; (2) to create an appreciation for God's creative genius; (3) to disprove modern theories of evolution.

Evangelism Aim—How can one teach this lesson to stress the need for personal salvation? What would drive home the basic truths of the gospel, leading to personal faith in Christ? Let us follow a line of reasoning that leads to an evangelism aim.

It is impressive to observe the magnitude of God's creative power. Perhaps the motif of creative power is the focal point of truth around which the message of personal salvation could be built. Since 2 Corinthians 5:17 speaks of salvation as creating a new person in Christ with old things passing away, and all things becoming new, it would be right to speak of God's power to create a new heart. Such a lesson aim could be stated as follows: "To know that Jesus will create a new heart in anyone who will allow Him entrance." This aim is good because it rises logically from the text, is concise, easily illustrated, and will naturally lead to an invitation to accept Christ as Savior.

THE EXODUS FROM EGYPT (Exodus 1 through 14)

Narrative—In Egypt, Jacob's family grew into a great nation. When a new Pharaoh came into power, he looked upon this foreign people as a threat to national unity. He began to persecute the Israelites with heavy labor assignments. God, who had chosen this nation to be His people, sent Moses to lead them to a new land of great opportunity. After God had spoken through many plagues upon Egypt, Pharaoh allowed God's people to leave. Attempts to bring them back failed, and God's people triumphed.

Possible Aims—(1) To prove the superiority of God's power over all other earthly power; (2) to show the bondage that comes through disobedience; (3) to demonstrate how God works all things together for good; (4) to show how God takes care of His own.

Evangelism Aim—How can this lesson be developed to stress the need for a personal commitment to Christ? What would be a lesson aim that guides the teacher's preparation and presentation in the direction of evangelism? Is there a basic truth, a motif, in the narrative that lends itself to a salvation emphasis? If so, can it be illustrated easily? Will it be significant to the age-group?

One idea lies on the surface of the story—escape! By God's initiative, Israel was able to escape from bondage. Egypt speaks of the bondage of sin—the old life of imprisonment to self—and the journey out as the way of grace that leads to a new life. The following lesson aim will then be appropriate: "To describe the bondage caused by sin and to show that the only way to escape is to accept Jesus as Savior."

There are, of course, other aims that could be developed that would be considered evangelism aims. The important thing, however, is that the teacher discipline himself to be absolutely clear in stating the particular aim guiding the lesson. To leave this choice to the inspiration of the moment is to suppress the Holy Spirit's free work in directing both the preparation of the lesson and its presentation.

THE ADULTERY OF GOMER (Hosea 1 through 3)

Narrative—The Lord told Hosea to marry a woman of ill repute. After three children were born to Hosea and Gomer, Gomer began to desire the association of other men. She went from bad to worse, until eventually she became a slave. God gave Hosea an unquenchable love for Gomer. Finally, Hosea bought Gomer at the local slave market and took her home to be his wife once again.

Possible Aims—(1) To show the gradual decline caused by lustful living; (2) to trace the backslidings of Israel from one generation to another; (3) to demonstrate the qualities of a good father; (4) to explore ways of making our family strong.

Evangelism Aim—As with most stories in the Bible, there are many truths in the narrative that suggest the grace of God in salvation. The teacher must ask, "How can I point the lesson to gain the greatest response from the students? What aspect of the lesson should be particularly developed with the idea of opening the door to students' hearts so they may enter into a personal relationship with Jesus Christ?"

Here is an opportunity to dramatize the awful effects of sin, as typified in Gomer's experience. Here too is a beautiful picture of Christ, our heavenly Hosea, who paid the full price to redeem sinful man from a life of servitude to sin. This truth can be stated in the following lesson aim: "To show how sin has enslaved every man and that only the death of Christ can purchase his freedom."

A lesson aim is not restrictive or exclusive. Rather, it is designed to establish a mark toward which the essential parts of the lesson may point. Divergent lines of thought, a variety of illustrations, and interesting sidelights are all in order. They must, however, be directed toward the lesson's central goal and aim.

In teaching this lesson, it would be difficult to ignore any of the truths suggested above under "Possible Aims." They should be a vital part of the lesson, and the teacher can arrange and present them in such a way as to support the central aim of the lesson. This approach allows for the presentation of a breadth of material and yet it preserves the value of a pointed thrust through the main lesson aim.

THE SERMON ON THE MOUNT (Matthew 5 through 7)

Narrative—Whether Jesus spoke this sermon at one sitting or whether the gospel writers pieced it together from different discourses He gave is incidental. Seated on a hill, Jesus gathered His disciples to Him and began to teach them about life in the kingdom of God—or the life of discipleship. The sermon is a powerful treatise on Christian conduct. It measures true religion according to the heart, over against obedience to the law alone. This narrow way is called straight and hard. It is reserved, Jesus said, for the poor in spirit, the meek, those hungry and thirsty after righteousness, and the pure in heart. Dealing with such practical matters as divorce, anger, forgiveness, vows, and fasting, the Lord leaves little question about what is involved in living the true life of discipleship.

Possible Aims—(1) To show the contrast between internal faith and external religion; (2) to define discipleship as Jesus taught it; (3) to learn how to avoid religious hypocrisy; (4) to understand the culture of Jesus' day.

Evangelism Aim—This narrative presents a different kind of challenge from the others we considered. Jesus is directing His remarks to His disciples, those who already were following Him. How can a teacher develop evangelism aims from a text that is not directed to the unsaved?

Let us look at this passage. Locating a truth that suggests salvation is more difficult here. On the surface, it appears that lesson aims will necessarily be directed toward Christian maturity. A more careful examination reveals a good opportunity to point out the inadequacy of self-righteousness. Does not Jesus point out the ridiculous folly of all attempts at external religion? How can anyone be a disciple without first developing an allegiance to his Master? Consider then the following lesson aim: "To show how Jesus enters human personality and changes men from the inside out."

A later chapter will show how a lesson aim of this kind can be made highly personal. In all of the evangelism aims listed here, there has been no attempt to individualize them. This will be brought into focus later through a discussion of the invitation to accept Christ.

Pertinent Questions

1. *Must every lesson be slanted or aimed at the unsaved?*

Every class is strikingly different. Age-level is a consideration. The number in attendance is a determining factor. Rate of turnover and the regularity of visitor attendance are also a part of the composite. Some teachers feel that all members of their class are born again and, therefore, salvation lessons are not needed. Even if this appears to be the case, however, a sensitive teacher will realize that sometimes people play the part of being a Christian, yet have never really made a firm commitment to Christ. For the sake of such people, there should be an occasional salvation aim.

2. Can there be more than one central aim for a given lesson?

Curricular materials sometimes suggest several possible aims. Teachers may follow all of them in the course of lesson development. However, it is best for a teacher to state the lesson aim in his own words, and incorporate into that central aim the several other aims he feels have special significance.

Teachers will find a class responds best when the entire period moves in one particular direction. Numerous, scattered ideas are hard to assimilate and act upon. One central aim, with supportive secondary aims, will produce the best results. In some instances, when a class is largely composed of children an evangelism aim may be supportive to the central aim. The central aim of the lesson may concern discipleship, yet a supportive aim may stress the need for beginning the life of discipleship by personally receiving Christ.

This dual aim approach to lesson development and presentation is well stated by Wesley Willis:

> I have found that a good approach is to have two aims for each lesson. One of these could emphasize the principles which learners should know when the class is over. The second should indicate the type of behavior their newfound knowledge ought to produce.[5]

3. Is it equally important to structure lesson aims for children?

In the younger age-levels, play activities that are carefully directed will help to meet a lesson aim. If he defines that aim clearly, the teacher will be able to lead play activities to fulfill specific objectives. If the lesson aim is to teach children to love parents, a teacher may have the children roleplay parent and children activities to show how many ways children can show their love to their parents.

Summary

Is it not enough simply to teach the Bible and let the Holy Spirit make the application? On the surface, nothing could sound more biblical or more spiritual. Yet this reasoning is more often an excuse for laziness and indifference. Jesus taught with pointed words and with clear objectives. He was discriminating in all that He said, lest He be misunderstood and His teaching go afield.

The Holy Spirit wants to direct the teacher in each part of the teaching process. He will be present as much in the preparation as He is in the presentation. It is His specific ministry to pierce the human heart with truth, and He uses human instruments to do it. This calls for careful preparation and well-defined lesson aims—as the Spirit guides.

NOTES

[1]LeBar, 34.

[2]Lois E. LeBar, *Children in the Bible School* (Westwood, N.J.: Fleming H. Revell Company, 1952), 193.

[3]Findley B. Edge, *Teaching for Results* (Nashville, Tenn.: Broadman Press, 1956), 22–23.

[4]Clifford V. Anderson, "Evangelism in Christian Education," *Lamp*, July 1972 (National Sunday School Department), 7.

[5]Wesley Willis, *Make Your Teaching Count* (Wheaton, Ill.: Scripture Press, 1985), 129.

7
Controlling Classroom Atmosphere

Sue and Jim have just returned from their honeymoon and have eagerly anticipated their first Sunday in the young married couples' class. Only recently have they taken an interest in the church, and as yet are unsaved.

As Sue and Jim head for the designated classroom area, a glance at the clock reminds them that they are several minutes late. They are surprised, however, to find the classroom nearly empty and no teacher. No one welcomes them, and they sit close to the back of the room. The room is hot, poorly lighted, and obviously unkempt.

With nearly 10 minutes of the class period gone, the teacher finally arrives, hurriedly takes the roll, and plunges into the exposition of the lesson material. The context is good enough, but Sue and Jim wonder if a closed circuit television arrangement would be any less personal. The teacher alludes, in passing, to the importance of being converted. In the closing prayer, something is said about "those who would like to get saved."

Sue and Jim leave the classroom feeling that they could have spent their time in a more profitable manner.

The scenario described above is far too common in some of our churches. It is basically a problem of classroom atmosphere and spirit. Usually the situation can be rather easily remedied.

Physical Conditions

Take a mental walk through your Sunday school. Why are some rooms inviting, seeming to call people to stop and take a look? What makes other rooms drab and uninviting? Why does one room speak of activity and life, while another has an atmosphere of heaviness and inactivity?

Have you ever thought of the influence that atmosphere has upon your thinking and conduct? A softly lit restaurant suggests that you lower your voice without anyone requesting that you do so. A great cathedral prompts feelings of awe and reverence without any help from ushers or guides. A well-arranged supermarket will influence both the choice and the number of items you purchase. A bargain counter with commodities indiscriminately scattered about produces a totally different level of motivation for buying than does a well-ordered department store.

The same is true in the church. For example, a poorly lighted area creates a mood that does not contribute positively to a learning experience. Disheveled articles and supplies, dusty furniture, and unwashed chalkboards speak powerfully about the people who direct the Sunday school. These factors may seem trivial, but they contribute greatly to classroom atmosphere.

Another condition that may contribute negatively to classroom atmosphere is the matter of groupings. In smaller schools, closely graded classes may be impossible. However, leaders should structure the school to make the most of homogeneous groupings. When the age span is too broad, especially among children, the teacher will find it difficult to reach each end of the age spectrum. It is important that children, and adults as well, feel comfortable with the age span that comprises their class.

Adequate facilities do not necessarily have to be elaborate or new, although a new and modern structure has many advantages. Many older buildings have been inexpensively decorated and furnished to provide a good learning atmosphere. Both the exterior and interior of the church can have a facelift with a few gallons of paint. This inexpensive project can create a totally different atmosphere for the church and its activities. Add to this new curtains, a few yards of carpet, a light fixture with greater output and better maintenance, and the atmosphere of a classroom will be vastly improved.

What do facilities have to do with evangelism in the Sunday school? More than we may imagine. For example, the casual observer may conclude that our love for him is shallow, otherwise we would be more concerned about his comfort and enjoyment. Another may conclude insensitivity in physical things may also mean insensitivity in spiritual things. Whether these impressions are justified or not, the church must remove hindrances to learning and response and open more widely the door of opportunity for the lost.

Teacher Attitude

The teacher's attitude becomes the class' attitude. The spirit of the teacher becomes the spirit of the class. The teacher controls the classroom atmosphere. In other words, a Sunday school class reflects its teacher. If the teacher is schedule conscious, the members of that class will tend to arrive on time. If a teacher is prayerful, soon that quality will be apparent in the lives of the students. If a teacher has compassion for the lost, witnessing will be a priority for the members of that class. The Lord has set aside teachers as much for example as for instruction. Their positive influence and attitude can make the classroom atmosphere constructive, challenging, and inspiring.

What are the ingredients of positive teacher attitude as it relates to classroom atmosphere?

1. *Attendance to details*—It is the teacher's responsibility to be sure the classroom is adequately furnished, equipped, ventilated, lighted, and arranged. In most cases, others will be employed to do these tasks, but the ultimate responsibility is the teacher's. A wise teacher will find ways to do the best with what is available, working cooperatively with those who give overall direction to the Sunday school program. It is also the teacher's responsibility to be sure the time schedule for the class serves its students well, and that tardiness and absenteeism are controlled in a tactful and sensitive manner.

2. *Cheerfulness*—Jesus' promise to His disciples was that they would know true joy. When this attribute is clearly evident in the teacher, the students will be strengthened and challenged. Even when dealing with sin and exposing problems of carnality, there can still be an atmosphere of joy which centers in the adequacy of God's grace. The classroom is not the place for the parading of woes. The gospel is positive and must be shared in demonstration of the life and joy that Jesus gives.

3. *Sensitivity to good manners*—Students should never be embarrassed or made to feel uncomfortable. The classroom is not the place for encouraging arguments and settling touchy issues. Some teachers have used un-Christlike methods to achieve personal goals, but in the process have destroyed student confidence. The liberty of the Spirit is not a license for indiscriminate and embarrassing conduct. A wise teacher will be sensitive to his students' feelings and will seek to eliminate all approaches and attitudes that might produce restlessness and discontent. It is tragic if the gospel is rejected because of the teacher's attitude.

4. *Careful preparation*—Students are quick to detect either the shallowness or the depth of teacher preparation. An effective teacher does not forget that the students spend a considerable amount of time attending the class, and he owes them a quality of instruction that is indicative of careful preparation. There is no substitute for quality—and quality is directly related to preparation.

Jean Fisher speaks of the importance of teacher preparation in order to provide the maximum opportunity for learning:

> The teacher's careful planning and organization of the learners and materials (also) provide structure. Learners experience security in knowing how to work within the organizational structure of the classroom. Order and non-threatening control and an atmosphere permeated by the mutual respect of teacher and children relieves anxiety and frustration and allows everyone to concentrate on the work at hand.[1]

5. *Dependence on the Holy Spirit*—While the points men-

tioned above are important, nothing is so directly related to the classroom atmosphere as is the Holy Spirit's presence. Students must receive Bible truths on two levels: the mind and the heart. No matter how adequate the facilities, how well prepared the teacher, unless the Holy Spirit is present the defined goals of the class can never be attained.

Creativity and Class Atmosphere

Lawrence O. Richards discusses at some length the necessity of developing a creative atmosphere in the classroom.[2] He included in his book an outline for a creative teaching approach to Philippians and Colossians. In each instance Richards stresses the teacher's role as class director—guiding the students to their own discovery of Bible truth and the development of their own plan for its application in their personal lives. Interaction between individuals and within groups makes learning exciting and stimulating.

How can a teacher develop a creative atmosphere in the classroom?

1. *Dare to change*—Experiment with new methods and approaches to the lesson. While the traditional lecture method has its value, it may be stimulating for your class to break up into small groups and search together for the main truths of the lesson. Perhaps a brainstorming session would give the class members an opportunity for a personal response that would make each student feel a more vital part of the group.

2. *Use others*—Quite likely there are members of the class who possess special abilities and talents. Why not call on them periodically to supplement what you, as the teacher, are doing? An attorney would probably be happy to discuss the trial of Jesus from a legal point of view. A farmer could give insight into the metaphors Jesus used that come from the agrarian lifestyle of His day. A nurse could help the class understand the references in Luke's Gospel and the Book of Acts that point to Luke's medical background. A teenager could do a psychological study on the Prodigal Son to help the class understand

what factors produce the desire to run away from home. Using people's various areas of expertise will produce variety and creativity when properly directed by the teacher.

3. *Pray*—Asking the Lord for a creative mind is a valid prayer for the teacher. The Holy Spirit is not tied to one approach. A study of the life of Christ reveals great diversity. Jesus taught by declaration, by example, by parables, by allowing others to speak, by silence, and by rhetoric. Students will appreciate a teacher's sincere attempt to offer variety in approach.

Elements of Good Classroom Atmosphere

Lois E. LeBar points out four basic elements of good programming which in turn produce good classroom atmosphere. She cites Nehemiah 8 as a pattern.[3] When the people saw Ezra open the book and bless the Lord, they lifted their hands, bowed their heads, and worshiped (worship). The Levites then expounded the Scriptures so the people could understand (instruction). Following a time of instruction, the people were admonished to keep the Feast of Tabernacles (fellowship). Finally, the people were instructed to prepare their best food and share with those who could not afford a feast (expression).

1. *Instruction*—The Bible is the final source of authority and inspiration in the instructional process. The Bible tells man who he is, the nature of his problems, and his future destiny. It also tells man about God and His plan to redeem man and nurture him in His love. Regardless of age-level, the Sunday school class that does not find a focus in the Scriptures will miss its mark.

2. *Worship*—While instruction challenges the mind, it is worship that enriches the soul and spirit. David exclaimed, "One thing I ask of the Lord, this is what I seek: that I may dwell in the house of the Lord all the days of my life, to gaze upon the beauty of the Lord and to seek him in his temple" (Psalm 27:4, NIV).

True worship rarely occurs without preparation. The teacher must ask the Holy Spirit to assist in the selection of songs, the development of the lesson, the structure of lesson aims, and the delivery of the materials to create an atmosphere of worship. It may also be helpful to instruct the class members in how to worship God. While worship is basically a matter of the heart, some students could be greatly helped if they were taught to enter actively into worship.

3. *Expression*—It is not enough to learn from God's Word and to worship God. These experiences, though rich in themselves, must be followed by practical application.

> In 1792, in a Baptist chapel in Nottingham, England, William Carey preached on the text, "Lengthen thy cords and strengthen thy stakes." His outline was: attempt great things for God, expect great things from God. After the sermon, when the people filed out as usual, Carey cried in dismay to a friend, "Aren't we going to do anything? Oh, call them back, call them back! We dare not separate without doing anything!" Carey later went to India to become the first modern missionary.[4]

How often have hearts been blessed and challenged, but no plan emerged to channel that experience to the world.

4. *Fellowship*—Fellowship was a vital part of the Apostolic Church. The word to describe this fellowship is *koinonia*, which means sharing openly with others that which has been received. True fellowship is more than ice cream socials and church dinners. *Koinonia* speaks of a sharing experience that goes far deeper than material considerations. It suggests a unity of spirit, a common bond of love, a singleness of purpose, and an openness of heart. In this context, the reconciling work of Christ flows freely from one person to another. Sins are confessed, burdens are revealed, help is given, and the body of Christ is strengthened.

Class Atmosphere and Evangelism

How does class atmosphere relate to evangelism? Is there a link between right class atmosphere and true decisions for Jesus Christ? Do some students reject Christ simply because the atmosphere of the class has been distracting and insincere?

What factors can we isolate as conditions that encourage unbelievers to accept Christ as Savior?

1. *Love*—An atmosphere that is alive with love will draw the unsaved to Christ. In a world filled with hatred and loneliness, there will be a positive response to the genuine love of believers. However, the unsaved will not respond to love that condescends. But when love flows horizontally, noting all are in need of God's grace, the unbeliever will be touched by conviction. A class that emits this kind of love will be sought after by those in need of Christ.

2. *Friendliness*—Most people are looking for a kind of love that leads to friendship and social acceptance. None of us is a self-contained social unit, but rather we are very dependent upon good relationships with those around us. The church, then, must provide an atmosphere that makes people feel they really do belong. Occasional social gatherings, a preclass fellowship time, and personal visits will do a great deal to communicate friendliness. New converts frequently testify that it was the openness and warmth of a Sunday school class the Holy Spirit used to speak to them about salvation.

3. *Relevance*—The Bible is more than a book about life—it is life itself. The gospel is more than the story about life—it is life itself. It is exciting when a student comments, "I see the answer to my problem right here in the Word of God!" Jesus meets all of us right where we are, and then leads us on to be more like himself. When Jesus spoke to the woman by the well, to Nicodemus, and to the rich young ruler, it was at a juncture in their lives. He met them where they were. He related directly to their experience.

4. *Opportunity*—The class atmosphere encourages the unsaved to respond to the call of Christ. If the atmosphere is highly structured and somewhat impersonal, the one in need of Christ may feel there is no opportunity for him to make a clear decision for Christ. A less highly structured atmosphere will seem more personal and suggest to the inquirer that his need is important to the entire class.

Summary

It may be interesting to ask the members of your class what conditions the Lord used to draw them to himself. Some of the likely answers are: "I had a junior high teacher who loved me into the Kingdom." "Our pastor demonstrated a love and warmth that the Lord used to speak to my heart." "I just felt something different about this church—the atmosphere was different—and the Spirit used it to convict me of my sin."

A wise teacher will sit where his students sit and think seriously about the way they feel as they listen from week to week. Success or failure in teaching is largely a matter of atmosphere.

It is what people experience in their hearts that ultimately matters most.

NOTES

[1] Roy B. Zuck and Robert E. Clark, *Childhood Education in the Church* (Chicago: Moody Press, 1986), 292.

[2] Lawrence O. Richards, *Creative Bible Teaching* (Chicago: Moody Press, 1970), 78–99.

[3] LeBar, *Focus on People in Church Education,* 35–44.

[4] Ibid., 42.

8
Making the Invitation

This chapter falls naturally into three parts: (1) How to invite children to Christ; (2) How to invite youth to Christ; (3) How to invite adults to Christ. Each section will begin with a life situation, followed by an analysis of problems and a suggestion of solutions. It is hoped the teacher will discover practical suggestions here that will be helpful in leading students to a personal and enduring relationship with Christ. To a large degree, we have failed as Christian teachers if we do not see that the students under our care come directly to grips with the individual claims of Christ upon their lives.

Life Situation

Cindy is 5 and eagerly waiting for her first year in school to begin. She has been in Sunday school as long as she can remember. Cindy has responded to several invitations to accept Jesus as her Savior, yet is somewhat unsure of what it is all about. One time she is told to let Jesus into her heart, and the next time to give her heart to Jesus. Several weeks ago Cindy heard that all those who didn't want to go to hell should come forward to receive Jesus as Savior. She was afraid not to respond. Cindy wonders how many times she may go forward to get saved. Each time she has done something wrong she wonders if she must now get saved again. Cindy has also found it hard not to respond each time her teacher tells an emotional story and then asks everyone who wants to do so to come forward to receive Jesus. Unfortunately, Cindy and many of her friends are confused about what it really means to be saved.

Analysis

Why is there such clear evidence of confusion among children relative to accepting Christ as Savior? Reflecting on the life situation outlined above, several observations are in order.

1. *Children must be taught about salvation with words that are clear and meaningful to them.* A wise teacher will carefully choose words and phrases familiar to children and that accurately communicate the plan of salvation.

2. *Children should not be frightened into making a decision for Christ.* The threat of judgment and hell is a poor basis upon which to invite children to accept Christ. Soon the scary feeling wears off, but the residue of confusion lingers on.

3. *Children must be taught that once they have received Christ, His grace is sufficient to keep them.* It is regrettable that so many children do not have the full assurance of their salvation.

4. *Children must not be invited to receive Christ on the basis of personal reward.* Most children will gladly respond to an invitation if they feel it will produce special recognition or a gift of some particular interest. Rarely are such decisions fruitful. In fact, such an approach reduces the gospel to merchandise and leaves disappointment and confusion in its wake.

5. *Children must not be invited to receive Christ on an emotional basis alone.* It is not difficult to cause children to weep in response to a touching story with which they can easily identify. However, if children respond only because their emotions are stirred, their supposed spiritual experience will leave as the emotional feeling leaves.

6. *Children must be dealt with individually.* It is wrong to expect that a group of children will come collectively to Christ in a meaningful way. Usually it takes a personal touch from someone who will deal pointedly and specifically with a child who has responded.

Bible Content and the Invitation

In an earlier chapter we said that meaningful decisions for

Christ presuppose the understanding of certain biblical truths. This is also true with respect to children. A child's response should be directly related to an understanding of the Word of God. It may be his understanding is extremely limited, and his concept of divine revelation is quite immature. Yet the decision must be based upon the Bible content present in the mind and heart of the child.

Marjorie Soderholm suggests the following Bible truths that must undergird a child's decision for Christ:

1. God loves you.
2. You have sinned.
3. Christ died to pay for your sins.
4. You must admit to Him that you are a sinner and ask Him to forgive you.
5. Then you are in God's family and you have everlasting life.[1]

Without some understanding of these basic truths, it is unlikely a child can have a conversion experience that will stand the test of time. Most teachers have been amazed at how early in life a child may grasp these truths if they are stated in terms the child understands.

There are many groups of verses which the teacher may use to establish a foundation for decision. John 3:16 gives a good background to the plan of salvation and is usually familiar even to young children. Isaiah 53:6 and Romans 3:23 establish the lost condition of every man. John 3:36 contains the promise of everlasting life. While the teacher may not choose to quote Scripture verses verbatim, he should follow the thought progression of such groups of verses. It cannot be overemphasized that a child's decision must be as solidly based on the Word as is the decision of an adult.

Questions and the Invitation

It is important that the teacher allow the students to ask questions. These questions will serve as a guide to indicate the depth of student comprehension. Following is a typical series of questions and answers that lead naturally to the invitation:

QUESTION: What is sin?
ANSWER: Sin is disobeying God.
QUESTION: Have I sinned?
ANSWER: Yes, you have sinned by your thoughts and actions.
QUESTION: What can I do about my sin?
ANSWER: You can ask Jesus to forgive you.
QUESTION: How can He forgive my sin?
ANSWER: Because He died to pay the price for your sin.
QUESTION: How can I be forgiven by Jesus?
ANSWER: By telling Jesus you are sorry for your sins and believing in Him to forgive you.

In each instance the teacher needs to take care that his answers are simple but true. Observe that these answers can be easily built upon with additional information.

The teacher must not only be willing to hear the questions the students ask, but he must also be able to ask the right questions. Children want to participate, to be a part of the action, to feel that something is happening, that they are included. Children like to answer questions. Effective teachers will use this method as a guide in lesson development and in the method and timing of the invitation.

Stories and the Invitation

Marjorie Soderholm suggests the following three questions to determine if a story is appropriate to be used in leading children to Christ:

1. Do the words mean what they say?
2. Is the story free from fanciful ideas?
3. How much of the story is actually the Word of God?[2]

Think about many of the typical object lessons used in children's meetings. Is it possible that jumping beans, black clothes, ink blots, and other such objects might conceal biblical truth rather than reveal it? Is it possible that elaborate stories that depend primarily on suspense and drama, may create false impressions?

Teachers should become skilled in relating Bible stories so they effectively explain the plan of salvation. The conversation between Jesus and Nicodemus recorded in John 3, cannot be improved upon as a model of what Jesus is asking of each of us. When Jesus met the woman of Samaria at the well, the drama of salvation unfolded in a most fascinating way. Children will stand by to watch as Paul and Silas lead the Philippian jailer to a personal faith in Christ. Of course, object lessons can be profitably used, but a well-told and carefully illustrated Bible story will do much to make God's plan of salvation understandable to children.

It is important too that those who teach children develop a sensitivity to the correct interpretation and use of Scripture. If children are exposed to a careless and inaccurate handling of the Scriptures, it will be difficult for them to become good students of the Word as they mature into adulthood. For this reason those who teach children should be especially careful that their approach to the Bible, although expressed on an elementary level, reflect good methods and principles of Bible study. (For example, stating that "God is just like Santa Claus, because the Bible says that He is the giver of every good and perfect gift," creates a false image and attributes to the Bible an idea it really does not state.)

The Spirit's Work in Conviction

A well-told Bible story, carefully developed illustrations, and friendliness and warmth are all ingredients of a good classroom setting, but these alone will not produce converts. It is the Spirit's ministry that confirms the Word, exalts Jesus Christ, and convicts of sin. Only by His work will children make enduring commitments to Christ.

How does a teacher recognize the presence of the Holy Spirit in conviction? What are the evidences of conviction? Are there certain conditions that produce conviction? Following are some basic principles.

1. *Be willing to stop at any point in the class period to pray with and guide those who are being convicted of sin by the Spirit.* There is often a right time for a child to give his heart to Christ, and to delay may mean that opportunity is lost.

2. *Explain how the Spirit works in conviction.* Children are information seekers; they need to have their curiosity satisfied. They will be more apt to respond to the Holy Spirit if they have been instructed as to how He works in their lives.

3. *Watch for outward signs of the presence of conviction.* Children sometimes, although not always, become unusually serious and reflective. They may even shed tears, as the Holy Spirit speaks to them. An effective teacher is alert to these outward signs.

4. *Listen for indications of conviction, both in the questions children ask and the answers they give to questions the teacher asks.* Following are questions that are typical of those asked by children when the Holy Spirit is at work in conviction: "What do I need to do to go to heaven?" "Will I be lost if I don't ask Jesus to forgive me?" "How long is eternity?" "Where will I go when I die?" "How can I be sure I won't go to hell?" Obviously, these questions could be asked only out of curiosity, but often they point out a sincere desire to respond positively to the work of the Holy Spirit.

Leading a Child to Christ

Thus far we have spoken about the need for evangelism in the classroom, good principles of communication, using language that is meaningful, preparing the lesson for decision, and creating classroom atmosphere to encourage decision. What about the crucial time when the Holy Spirit has prepared a child's heart and you as teacher must direct that child to Christ in a specific way? What is your role in leading that child to a decision that will last for eternity?

Following are several principles for the guidance of the teacher in effectively using this opportunity to lead a child to Christ.

1. *State clearly and simply what it means to come to Christ for salvation.* Avoid using any kind of gimmickry. Be forthright. Allow the Spirit to guide you as you explain clearly what it means to come to Christ in salvation.

2. *Be personal and individualistic.* This is one reason why every class should have more than one adult on the teaching team. A time of personal prayer in a private place is essential. Any questions the child asks at this point should be carefully and thoroughly answered.

3. *Use the Bible.* Even children need the authority of the Scriptures to explain the how and why of their decision to accept Christ. Although these verses may have been referred to during the class period, it is necessary at the time of decision for a child to "see it for himself" in the Scriptures. It may be wise for the child to read those verses audibly.

4. *Guide the child's emotions.* A child may be under deep conviction and so moved that his sobbing prevents meaningful prayer and guidance. While we must be careful not to hinder what the Spirit is doing, it is often helpful to suggest that a child stop weeping in order to receive instruction and help. The emotional feelings will soon leave, and the child must recall a decision made with his mind and will, as well as his emotions. One reason why some children do not mature in their walk with Christ is because they had only an emotional experience at the time they came to Christ.

5. *Explain what has happened.* In the next chapter we will say more about the matter of assurance, but it is important to stress here the need for building a support base that will sustain that new experience. A wise teacher will help the child understand that God will not break His promise, that his position before God is secure, and that the Holy Spirit will provide keeping power.

When a child comes from a non-Christian home, special help is essential. The indifference of his unsaved parents can be most discouraging to a child who has just come to Christ. This is another reason why it is so important for teachers to understand the home backgrounds of the children they teach. Some parents will not only be unsympathetic to a child's conversion experience; they may openly oppose it. That child must be as prepared as possible for such oppositions.

Life Situation

Don has taught the high school class for several years. The class has shown genuine interest in Bible study, and Don has been thankful for a steady numerical growth. More recently, however, Don has sensed that several members of the class are unsaved. As he sits down to prepare next Sunday's lesson, he cannot help but think about these students. Several questions come to mind as the lesson begins to unfold: (1) How can I supply the lesson to these students so they will sense their need for Christ? (2) How will I know that the Holy Spirit is at work to convict of sin? (3) How can I make an invitation that will press for commitment but not embarrass them before their friends?

Analysis

Don's burden is that of many who work with youth. In most youth classes there are some who are very much a part of class activities but have never had a specific confrontation with Christ that has resulted in personal faith. Reflecting on the life situation outlined above, several observations may be helpful.

1. *Young people must have a personal and life-changing experience in Jesus Christ.* Some youth leaders have been satisfied with student loyalty and curiosity, and have not stressed the need for a personal experience with Christ. A student may have a keen interest in the Scriptures, a flawless attendance record, and a cooperative spirit and still not be truly born again.

2. *Young people are sensitive about peer acceptance.* To be popular with the gang is a top priority with many young people.

This psychological phenomenon can be used to good advantage if the class atmosphere is such that young people feel a genuine spiritual responsibility for one another.

3. *Young people thrive on challenge.* Young people will accept the Bible at face value. A watered-down gospel is not to their choosing. A teacher who courageously presents the challenge of discipleship, the life of surrender, and the call to evangelize will usually find acceptance. Young people are sensitive about hypocrisy. They will appreciate a teacher who comes across as openly honest and forthright.

4. *Young people are open to influence.* The direction of their lives is not yet crystallized. They are looking for direction. Later in life, change is made only with a great deal of effort. What an opportunity to demonstrate to youth the joy of living for Christ!

Pointing the Lesson To Reach Youth

How can a teacher present the lesson so unsaved young people will be drawn to Christ? Following are general principles that will help him in this challenging responsibility.

1. *Teach from clearly defined lesson aims.* This was dealt with in detail in an earlier chapter. It is adequate here to stress again that student decision is directly related to lesson aims and goals. A lesson aim stressing personal commitment to Christ will often result in the unsaved coming to Christ.

2. *Teach from the heart.* A highly successful high school teacher accepted the assignment to teach more out of a desire and burden than out of ability and experience. But when he taught, his students knew he spoke from a concern and a burden born of love and compassion. Young people will respond when the lesson is presented with inspiration and feeling. They need to know that their teacher cares.

3. *Teach with understanding.* The so-called generation gap is bridged by adult workers who take the time to understand young people. Advanced technology, with rapid means of communication, has pushed young people to adult levels at an

earlier age. Television, for example, brings world events to young people in color and sound. The result is simply that young people grow up more rapidly. The teacher must face this reality and direct his challenge accordingly.

Young people live in a world of experience. Their music, art, and literature are designed to produce an experience. In this sense, theirs is a sensual world, a world that reaches out to stimulate their senses. Imagine a rock concert. The eyes pick up the lights, colors, and designs; the ears pick up the relentless and persistent beat and rhythm; and the entire body feels the pulsations of the energized atmosphere. The youth of today are the products of an experience-oriented society. The church must use this opportunity to preach the power of Christ to transform lives and the wonders of an authentic encounter with Jesus Christ. Nothing less than a gospel of power will touch youth.

4. *Teach on their level.* An effective teacher will strive to understand the world of young people. He will make an effort to become acquainted with their language, music, philosophy of life, recreational habits, and many temptations. Young people sense very quickly whether or not a teacher understands and whether or not the message is relevant to their lives. Many times conviction comes because the Lord has led a teacher to speak pointedly about sin and the needs of young people that arise out of the world in which they live.

5. *Teach for response.* Anticipate that the Holy Spirit is at work. Expect that lives are being touched by the Word as it goes forth. Pray that each thought will be directed by the Spirit to produce a positive response in young hearts. If teachers present lessons in a perfunctory and matter-of-habit manner, students sense it and may close their hearts to what the Lord would want to do. How much better when the atmosphere is charged with expectation—"This is a day of decision."

Recognizing the Presence of Conviction

How can a teacher recognize when young people are under the conviction of the Holy Spirit? Children are more obvious in this regard. They unashamedly show their emotions. But young people don't want to be "put on the spot." They resent being singled out. However, there are two principles that may serve as a guide in this respect.

1. *The Lord has promised to confirm His Word.* It is the Spirit that is at work. Whether that work is obvious and external or concealed and private, is of little consequence. To assume that tears, or some other sign, must accompany conviction is wrong. The important thing is that the Spirit is at work.

2. *Be sensitive to the Holy Spirit.* A Spirit-filled teacher will sense the work of the Holy Spirit in young lives. This leading must direct the course of events that will lead young people to a public confession of Christ as Savior. Damage can be done when older adults try to press young people into a salvation experience. This is a delicate matter, and only by the Spirit's leading can a teacher know how to proceed in helping a young person receive Christ.

Making the Invitation

Don has nearly completed the lesson. The Holy Spirit has enabled him to speak with clarity and authority. It is clear that hearts are touched. Don knows he cannot dismiss the class without giving an opportunity to respond to the message of salvation. But how? What should be done next? Will he embarrass the students and quench the work of the Spirit? While the Spirit leads in many different ways, we can make several recommendations.

1. *Explain thoroughly and honestly how you feel the Spirit is leading.* Much possible embarrassment will be avoided if the entire class knows what you feel led to do. Be careful to avoid any approach that may be deceptive. Don't put young people on the spot. Nothing will quench the Spirit more rapidly.

2. *Stress the need for prayer.* While a public confession is necessary, it is not an end in itself. With confession of sin should come an opportunity for personal and private prayer.

3. *Be flexible.* There is a time for asking students who feel drawn by the Spirit to raise their hands and indicate this. There are other times when a call to prayer for the entire class would be most helpful. On still other occasions a time of sharing may be the opportunity for a student to rise and publicly declare his new faith in Christ. The Holy Spirit must lead the teacher in directing this most important step.

4. *Be understanding.* It is important to lead a person step-by-step to an acceptance of Christ. Insensitivity here could quench the Spirit and drive that young person further into sin and rebellion. Tragedies have occurred when young people have been pushed into an experience that has been premature and, therefore, disappointing.

Life Situation

The Andersons have been leaders in the community for years. They're known for their honesty and integrity. In addition to their undertaking many civic responsibilities, the Andersons are recognized as good church people. Although their church is more socially oriented, they have given and worked for its growth and development. Following a crisis in their family, the Andersons accepted a neighbor's invitation to attend the local Assembly of God. They are now regular attenders, but as yet they are unsaved. Both the adult Bible teacher and the pastor are praying earnestly for their salvation.

Analysis

To ignore adult evangelism is to miss one of the church's greatest opportunities. Although many people make a decision for Christ during their younger years, it must never be assumed that adults are somehow beyond the reach of the gospel. Sometimes the old adage, "You can't teach an old dog new tricks," is mistakenly applied to adult evangelism. The Holy Spirit, however, is at work in every heart, regardless of age. Following are some general observations about adult evangelism.

1. *The biblical pattern of evangelism begins with adults!*

Several very significant questions need to be faced. Who were those who were reached for Christ when the New Testament Church came into being, and who formed its nucleus—children, youth or adults? How were those adults reached—through their children and youth, or by direct confrontation with the Gospel? Who throughout the scriptural record (in both the Old and New Testaments) were basically responsible for the spiritual nurture of children and youth—the religious leaders or parents? ... Christian education in the Bible focuses on adults who in turn were responsible to educate their children. Those first saved were adults, and those first trained and equipped to serve Christ were adults. The implication is clear: an adult reached for Christ and built up in faith resulted in entire families being reached for Christ and taught in Him.[3]

2. *Adults who are won to Christ usually continue to serve Him.* Unfortunately, many children drift away from their commitment during adolescent years. Adults, on the other hand, are more mature in their thinking, and when they make a decision to live for Christ it is usually a firm and abiding one. With this fact in perspective, adult evangelism is seen as a most fruitful area of ministry in the local church.

3. *Adults find it hard to change.* On the negative side, adults find it far more difficult to change their thinking and manner of living than do young people. Life habits and styles have become so much a part of experience as to make change very difficult. It is difficult for an adult to admit he has not lived right for the first 30 years of life. It is difficult to face a multitude of friends who have known the kind of life that was formerly lived. It is difficult to start over when so much of life is already past. Yet many adult converts testify to the adequacy of God's grace to bring about both a total transformation, and then the strength to bring their lives into conformity to that decision.

Helping an Adult To Receive Christ

Let's return to the Andersons. What suggestions will help

the teacher bring this couple to a personal experience with Jesus Christ?

1. *Develop confidence.* Adults are naturally more skeptical than young people. They need to feel confident that their teacher is worthy of their trust. To establish this confidence, personal contact is most fruitful. A friendly, warm relationship will generate the confidence a teacher needs to win another adult to Christ.

2. *Lay the groundwork.* A wise teacher will carefully explain what the Scriptures say about man's need for salvation. Biblical terminology and doctrine will be explained in a clear and practical way. Human need and divine provision will be brought together in a logical sequence. Adults will need to understand what salvation means before they will open their hearts to the Holy Spirit's influence.

3. *Recognize the presence of conviction.* Adults must come to Christ in exactly the same way as youth and children. There will be a time when people like the Andersons will be moved upon by the Holy Spirit to come to Christ. The teacher must sense this special moment and by the Spirit's help lead them to Christ. This time may be at the conclusion of a given lesson, in the home, or at a class social. At that moment, the teacher must be ready to encourage decision.

4. *Answer questions thoroughly.* Following are typical questions or comments adults express as the Spirit begins to work.

"I live a good life—as good as anyone else."

"I'm a good church member. I've been baptized and confirmed... I even support the church."

"I don't want to be a hypocrite!"

"Will Christ forgive what I've done?"

The teacher must carefully answer each inquiry from the Scriptures and not move on to another consideration until that inquiry is answered satisfactorily.

5. *Don't insult or embarrass.* Adults are very sensitive about matters they deem personal. To pressure or threaten will often quench the Spirit. Be kind, yet persistent—the task is of eternal

consequence and must not be taken lightly. When the Holy Spirit leads the teacher to make a public invitation at the conclusion of the class period, the teacher should take great care to explain how the invitation will be given, how a student may respond, and, most of all, what the Scriptures say about the importance of making a public confession of Christ. As with youth, any kind of gimmick or subtle technique to gain response will lead to disappointing results. Let the Spirit work, and there is then no need for pressure. When the Spirit has done the work, the decision will be sound and Christ will be glorified.

NOTES

[1] Soderholm, 10–11.
[2] Ibid., 16.
[3] Roy B. Zuck and Gene A. Getz, eds., *Adult Education in the Church* (Chicago: Moody Press, 1970), 5–6.

9
Reinforcing the Decision

Why does the church lose a high percentage of its youth?
Why does a new convert so quickly slip back into sin?
What is the spiritual mortality rate in the Sunday school where you teach?

These are just a few of the questions that come to mind when we face the matter of reinforcing those decisions that have been made for Christ. Most churches must admit to a shocking loss factor. Many who have had a vibrant testimony of salvation forsake that commitment and drift back into sin. The church must ask, "Why?"

However, the loss factor is not the only area of concern. What about the children, for example, who repeatedly answer invitations for salvation because they are afraid that if they don't they will be lost? What about young people who live in almost continual fear that by some act of disobedience they will be forever cut off from the grace of God? And what about adults who have never accepted the total redemptive work of Christ on their behalf, and therefore never do enter into that place of joy that comes with true assurance? Again, the church must ask, "Why?"

Doctrinal Considerations

Unfortunately, the doctrine of assurance has been stretched out of shape by theological controversy down through the centuries. Reformers John Calvin and Jacobus Arminius viewed salvation and assurance from two distinct points of view. Calvin emphasized the absolute security of a believer, while Arminius emphasized the daily walk with Christ as the foundation for assurance. Since the Reformation days believers have found themselves at some point along the continuum that stretches between Arminianism and Calvinism.

Some believers, claiming allegiance to John Calvin, have laid great stress on the security of the believer, while failing to emphasize the responsibility of abiding in Christ. Other believers, claiming to be followers of Arminius, have laid such stress upon personal responsibility that the grace of God in Christ has been diminished in their teaching.

Obviously, the truth lies between the two extremes. On the one hand, the believer must accept his positional relationship to God through Jesus Christ. This relationship is rooted in the redemptive plan of God and, as such, is secure. On the other hand, the believer has a responsibility to abide in Christ in a consecrated relationship through which God's keeping grace may flow. Assurance, therefore, has two essential components. First, there is the security of God's grace in Christ. Second, is an abiding relationship with Jesus Christ.

A Scriptural Analysis

It will be helpful to draw from the Scriptures statements that deal with the believer's security in Christ. Consider the following passages: John 10:28,29; Philippians 1:6; 2 Thessalonians 3:3; 2 Timothy 1:12; and 1 Peter 1:5. In each instance the emphasis is on the absolute and irreversible security of the believer whose life is hidden in Christ with God. In this abiding relationship there is final and complete assurance. It is this truth that must undergird a new convert as he begins his walk with Christ. As the Christian hymn so appropriately puts it, "How firm a foundation, ye saints of the Lord, Is laid for your faith in His excellent Word!"

It is also imperative for believers to recognize that their security is found only through an abiding relationship with Christ. The following Scriptures make this clear: 1 Corinthians

9:27; Hebrews 6:4–6; 10:26–29; and 2 Peter 2:20. Here the emphasis is upon the believer's responsibility to live a life in keeping with the Word and built upon a fellowship relationship with Christ. Great harm has been done to the work of God when either of the above emphases has been treated lightly. Conversely, believers have grown strong as they have learned to rely on Christ's power to keep them as they live a life of obedience and trust.

It is clear from the Scriptures that a believer's security is not destroyed by those occasions of incidental sin that come by virtue of a believer's imperfection, nor is it destroyed by momentary feelings of distrust or disobedience. The Lord knows the weaknesses of the flesh, and as a loving Father He looks with compassion and forgiveness upon those who are of a penitent spirit. A travesty is incurred upon the grace of God when believers come repeatedly for salvation, as if they have lost out with God, when all they need to do is look to Christ who is our ready Advocate with the Father.

Teaching Children About Assurance

"Daddy, I don't feel saved!"
"How come at night I always worry about being lost?"
"Will we go to heaven together some day?"
"Will heaven be fun?"

These questions, and many others, are familiar to Christian parents and children's workers. Children are security conscious, and they need to be assured that salvation is rooted in the character of God and will not come and go as emotions change. Children comment that they sometimes don't feel saved. Such thinking must be corrected. Salvation is not a matter of feelings; it is a contractual agreement that is backed by God's sovereign will as revealed in His Word.

There are several principles that serve to guide those who work with children in helping to reinforce their decisions to serve Christ.

1. *Show children in the Bible that salvation is sure.* It is good

to ask children to read aloud a specific passage that deals with assurance. A child who is troubled over the question of assurance will show great relief when the promises of God that deal with the believer's security are put solidly in place. It may be helpful to mark assurance passages in a child's Bible and suggest that he read those verses regularly. Nothing is so convincing as the Word of God—even to a child.

2. *Explain the treachery of human emotions.* A child needs to be taught that feelings are quite incidental to personal salvation. The will is more powerful than the emotions, and emotions will eventually catch up with the decisions of the will. A teacher may confidently ask the child to ignore certain emotions of fear, and rest instead upon the certainty of a decision he made with his will. It is time well spent to explain this principle to children. Unfortunately, some adults who have been Christians for years still try to find security in Christ based on emotional feelings. Christianity is a confessional religion; that is, God has promised to honor a confession of faith in Christ's redemptive work. This is the basis of biblical salvation.

3. *Seek to reinforce the conversion experience regularly.* A teacher should not hesitate to discuss the matter of assurance quite openly. This is a good time to emphasize that specific sins or momentary failures do not mean that salvation is lost. Sometimes a child tells a lie, becomes angry, or uses unbecoming language and feels sure that consequently he has lost his salvation. This is not true. While sin is to be taken very seriously and acts of transgression dealt with pointedly, children must see their salvation as rooted in God's love and indestructible so long as the abiding relationship with Christ is maintained.

4. *Develop the right concept of God.* The medieval concept of an angry, vengeful God has found its way into the thinking of some people. God is not waiting for a chance to denounce one of His children and erase that name from the Book of Life! God is a Father whose love will never let us go. As we strive to please Him, although out of weakness and occasional failure, God's grace remains adequate. He will not deny us.

Teachers and parents should be careful not to transmit a false concept of the nature of God by using Him as a threat. "If you do this, God will punish you!" It is true God disdains all sin, but using God as a threat makes Him a tyrant instead of a loving Heavenly Father. A true father seeks to maintain a relationship with a wayward son long after that son has broken ties with home. We need to show children that God is even more compassionate than an earthly father.

All of this is said not to minimize the importance of training children about the tragic consequences of sin. It is, instead, an appeal for correct thinking about God's basic nature. It is worth noting that wrong concepts taught to children will probably become wrong concepts retained in their thinking and experience when they become adults.

Introducing Water Baptism

A part of reinforcing the decision for Christ is to encourage new converts to be baptized in water. Although discipleship begins at the moment of conversion, water baptism marks that point in time for the world. During the first century, the persecutors of the Christians didn't ask "When were you saved" but "Have you been baptized?" Jesus gave the command to be baptized in the name of the Father, Son, and Holy Spirit to establish a point in time when the world would know that a sinner had come to repentance and was now willing to take the name of Jesus at any cost.

For the convert, however, water baptism is more than a public testimony of an inward decision. It marks, by symbolism, a total identity with Jesus Christ. Many have found in water baptism an avenue of spiritual power that has given them additional strength to serve Christ. A convert identifies with Christ in His death, symbolized by going down into the water, and with His resurrection, symbolized by coming out of the water. It is this experience that has served as a source of great blessing and encouragement to new converts.

When should a child be baptized in water? Many children

comprehend the basic plan of salvation at an early age and are truly saved. It may be, however, that these children are hardly ready for water baptism. A time of growth may be required before a child is able to appreciate baptism's full significance. There is, however, an equal danger in delaying water baptism beyond a reasonable time and robbing the child of a great potential for spiritual growth. Parents and teachers should cooperate in trying to determine the appropriate time for a child to be baptized in water. A good indication of readiness is the child's own request to be baptized. With proper guidance, this request can result in a most meaningful experience.

When should adult converts be baptized? There are two schools of thought relative to adult baptism. One suggestion is that new converts need to be instructed in the basic principles of the Christian life and demonstrate the same by being allowed to be baptized. On foreign mission fields especially, this has been a necessary practice.

Another position is that adult converts should be baptized immediately upon being saved. Some churches go from the altar service to the baptismal service. A new convert is baptized immediately, with only a brief time of instruction as to its meaning. The argument here is that immediate baptism seals the decision and opens the door to spiritual growth. The advocates of this position point out the immediate baptism of the Ethiopian eunuch as an example. Again, there is value in letting the request of the convert determine the time of baptism. At any rate, the command to be baptized must be taken most seriously, and every convert must be encouraged to enter into this experience.

Introducing Spirit Baptism

The Lord has granted to every believer the Holy Spirit. Without His presence there can be no conversion experience. But the Lord has also promised to every believer a Spirit baptism which is subsequent to conversion and marks the receiving of the Spirit in a fuller measure. Whether this experience is called the "infilling of the Spirit," the "baptism in the Spirit," or the "baptism in fire," each of the terms is used to point to the same basic experience. The disciples were instructed to wait in Jerusalem until the Spirit should fall in power. From the Upper Room emerged a group of Spirit-filled believers who went out to change the world by the power of the gospel. It is essential that every believer receive that same experience that came to the disciples assembled on the Day of Pentecost.

As converts are brought into the fellowship of the church, they should be led quite naturally into the baptism in the Holy Spirit. With some instruction, a new convert is ready to enter into this experience and should be encouraged to do so without delay. The infilling of the Spirit will do a great deal to reinforce the salvation decision and open the door to greater avenues of spiritual blessing and service. May we see a revival of emphasis upon being filled with the Spirit!

When should children be encouraged to receive the baptism in the Spirit? Once again, we are faced with a set of variables that make time-setting impossible. So much depends upon the individual child—his grasp of the Scriptures, his growth in Christ, and his basic desire to be filled. Since the Spirit is sovereign and moves as He wills, it is best to encourage children, at an appropriate time, to open their hearts and ask for the Spirit to come. However, there is some instruction to be given.

1. *The infilling of the Spirit comes as a gift.* It is received, not earned. Like salvation, it is claimed on the basis of faith, not works.

2. *The infilling of the Spirit is not necessarily a demonstrative or highly emotional experience.* Some children have received it in a very simple manner, yet their subsequent life has indicated that the experience was authentic. Adults need to be careful that they do not seek to impose upon children an experience like their own. Encouragement is always in order, but it is the Lord who fills. Tragically, some children have been pushed through to an apparent baptism in the Spirit and then

later in life have realized that the experience of their childhood was not the true work of the Spirit.

3. *The infilling of the Spirit must be thoroughly explained from the Word.* Obviously, this presupposes a certain level of intellectual and spiritual maturity on the part of the child. Children must understand that the baptism in the Spirit is solidly anchored in the Scriptures. Adults would do well to help a child understand both the nature of the experience and the simple faith and obedience that its receiving demands. Many adults look back and wonder why someone did not tell them how to yield simply to the Spirit and receive a lovely gift that God has given in Jesus Christ.

4. *The infilling of the Spirit is for power to be like Christ.* It is not only a point-in-time crisis experience; it is a process of spiritual growth that produces Christlikeness and victorious Christian living. Nothing is so practical as the Spirit-filled life. The presence of the Spirit provides the divine energy to create the attributes of Jesus Christ in the believer's heart. The dynamic life of service, therefore, is a logical and natural consequence of the Spirit-filled and Spirit-controlled life. Some people have erred in seeking a power for service, without having first recognized the Spirit's inner work to produce Christlikeness in attitude and conduct. The life of doing must follow the life of being.

How may adults be encouraged to receive the baptism in the Holy Spirit? In many of our congregations there are a number of fine Christian people who have never experienced the fullness of the Spirit. Some have grown weary of seeking. Some fear an emotional experience that will somehow embarrass them, and others simply do not desire the experience. Several observations may be helpful.

1. *The scriptural basis for the baptism in the Spirit must be clearly understood.* Ignorance breeds fear and reluctance. Some adults have never searched the Word for themselves to discover how helpful this experience is.

2. *The baptism in the Spirit cannot be stereotyped.* The Spirit is sovereign. He fills as He chooses. Man is only the yielded vessel. An adult who resists the work of the Spirit because there is a hesitancy to receive as others have received misses the personal nature of the Spirit's work. Again, not every adult will have a highly emotional experience. Not every adult needs to tarry for lengthy periods of time to be filled. Nor may it be necessary that the experience be received at the altar with friends gathered around in prayer. Many have been gloriously filled while at work, at home, in their car, and so on. Adults need to be reminded that the Spirit is at work, and they must yield in anticipation that at any time their experience may be brought into fullness.

3. *Let the Spirit do His work.* Since Jesus is the Baptizer, He is well able both to fill a vessel and produce the evidence of His presence. It is good to help a believer who is waiting to be filled to praise and worship. However, it is unscriptural and harmful to use pressure and constraint by trying to do what only the Spirit can do. Some adults have found it very difficult to yield to the Spirit because someone has, in misdirected zeal, attempted to assist the Spirit by using mechanical and human means of accomplishing spiritual goals. It does not work.

4. *Demonstrate the practical value of being filled with the Spirit.* It is the Holy Spirit's ministry to exalt Jesus Christ. Every believer needs a fullness of the Spirit, quickened daily, to produce in him the likeness of Jesus Christ. As adults observe the love of Christ and the grace of the Lord evident in the body of believers, they will desire the same fullness of Spirit presence. How tragic when adults confess that the daily evidences of the Spirit's fullness are not recognizable in those who claim to be filled with the Spirit. This condition calls for repentance.

Introducing the Lord's Supper

A new convert will also find strength in the Communion service. In the celebration of the Lord's death and resurrection,

114 / TEACHING FOR DECISION

there is a joining with Christ and with other believers through the corporate, symbolic partaking of the body and blood of Christ. The decision to serve Christ is strengthened and reinforced by participation in this service.

When should children be encouraged to participate in the Communion service? Here, again, much depends upon the child's spiritual maturity. Some children at ages 5 to 7 have a good understanding of salvation and could profit from the Communion service. Other children are much slower in grasping spiritual truths, and, for them, more time is needed before this service can be meaningful.

Parents and children's workers should watch for indications that a child is ready to participate profitably in the Communion service. It is not difficult to determine spiritual readiness if children's workers and parents will listen carefully to a child's comments and questions. Just as it is an error to allow a child to participate in the Lord's Supper simply out of curiosity, so it is an error to restrain a child for too long a time. To do so may hinder spiritual growth and progress.

Adult converts will be ready almost immediately to receive Communion. As with water baptism, the significance of the Lord's Supper can be quickly explained and participation made meaningful. Granted, there may be exceptions, but as a rule a new convert should be baptized in water and invited to participate in the Lord's Supper as soon as possible.

A Challenge

There is much that could be profitably said about spiritual growth and maturity. It is obviously a neglected area of concern in many churches. Following are subjects of interest to new converts as they seek to grow in grace:

1. The crucified life
2. The lordship of Jesus
3. The Spirit-controlled life
4. Living through times of temptation

5. Dealing with the carnal man
6. Going on to perfection

Each subject is worthy of fuller development. Salvation seen as process as well as event will focus attention on such areas of endeavor and development. As a baby must grow to live, so a new convert must continue to grow if he is to develop as a child of God.

10
Beyond the Classroom

A teacher's responsibilities and opportunities to evangelize do not end with the successful completion of the class period. Inevitably there will be those who will be won to the Lord at a variety of other times and places. An effective teacher will use these opportunities beyond the classroom to lead students to Christ as Savior. During a chance meeting in the park, on the way home from a church picnic, while visiting in the choir room after rehearsal, at a friend's birthday party—there are countless opportunities beyond the classroom. These must be used as the Spirit directs.

A Case in Point

It is extremely difficult for Brother Green to understand why he has had such meager success in reaching his adult students for Christ. Most of his students are born-again believers, but those who are not simply don't respond to the invitations he customarily gives at the conclusion of the class period. Brother Green carefully prepares each lesson. He prays earnestly for the unsaved members of his class. Yet, seemingly, it is to no avail.

The problem cited here persists at each age-level. Teachers are aware that needy souls are not coming to Christ, but they do not know what to do about it. The answer lies in an approach to evangelism that goes beyond the walls of the classrooms. It is the purpose of this chapter to single out several other key areas that provide an opportunity for evangelism.

Ministry to the Family

The family is the basic unit in society. When the family is strong, the community, the nation, and the church are strong. But when the family structure disintegrates, every facet of society suffers. The church must accept its responsibility to minister to the entire family. Unless it does so, it cannot hope to have an enduring ministry that will in turn build the kingdom of God. Every program of the local church should be directed in ministry to the needs of the entire family.

Larry Christenson points out the importance of the family by ascribing to it divine authorship.

> The family belongs to God. He created it. He determined its inner structure. He appointed for it its purpose and goal. By divine permission, a man and a woman may cooperate with God's purpose and become a part of it. But the home they establish remains His establishment. "Unless the Lord builds the house, those who build it labor in vain" (Psalm 127:1). The children receive their status as members of the family by His act. "God sets the solitary in families" (Psalm 68:6).
>
> Thus it is not our marriage, but His marriage; not our home, but His home; not our children, but His children; not our family, but His family.[1]

Starting from this premise, ministry to the family can hardly be considered optional. Granted, the Sunday school must be vitally concerned about individual growth and development, but it dare not ignore its responsibilities to the entire family. In some instances church calendars have placed so many demands on individual members of the family that it is impossible for them to enjoy enough time together as a family. The Sunday school must gear itself to strengthening individuals so they, in turn, can strengthen their family relationships.

How can the Sunday school minister to the entire family? It will be helpful, first, if teachers at each age-level will make a deliberate effort to present the biblical concept of the family. There is no substitute for knowledge, and correct knowledge about the family unit will help individuals to recognize their responsibilities in this regard. Second, it is wise for the teacher to become acquainted with the entire family. While close friendships are usually impossible on such a broad level, even a casual relationship with family members will prove helpful. Third, when possible, sponsor family activities, not only to strengthen intrafamily relationships, but to provide the opportunity for families to get together for fellowship and fun with other families.

How can ministry to the family produce decisions for Christ? The biblical pattern for evangelism centers in the family as a unit. In the Old Testament, children were taught the Scriptures by their parents. In the New Testament, the same emphasis is apparent. The Philippian jailer, for example, was won to Christ, and his entire household followed in that decision. It is good to reach children for Christ, but what about their parents? The biblical pattern is to win the parents and let them win the children. Obviously, when this process does not materialize, the church must then seek to win the children.

More pointedly, the home provides an excellent setting for a teacher to speak to a student about salvation. In this relaxed atmosphere it is often easy to move into a meaningful conversation about the plan of salvation. Teachers should not ignore the importance of contacts in the home.

The church should offer seminars, retreats, and conferences on family life. A noted youth leader commented that true revival begins with an awareness of spiritual responsibilities in the home. This being true, the church must do all it can to see that its families grow together in the harmony and love of the gospel.

Using the Altar Service

Next Sunday ask your students, "Where did you receive Christ?" Quite likely you will find that many decisions have been made at a church altar. Because this is true, we must face squarely the responsibility of the teacher in relation to the altar service.

It is a tragedy when a junior boy responds to an altar call on a Sunday evening, and his teacher is not present to help and encourage him in prayer. How incongruous for a teacher to pray and teach for student conversions and then miss those services when a personal response is likely to happen. Some churches have wisely established rigid requirements for Sunday school workers, including faithful attendance at church services. A teacher's presence says so much to his class members about the importance of faithfulness to the total ministry of the church and to the work of Jesus Christ.

However, a teacher's attendance is, in itself, not enough. A teacher should be a regular and personal participant in the altar service. If every Sunday school teacher would enter into the altar service with devotion of heart and spirit, imagine what it would do to strengthen the church and challenge others to seek the Lord! The members of the class need to see the importance of entering into group prayer and praise. Students will follow their teacher's example.

The altar service provides an excellent opportunity for counseling and sharing. When the Spirit is moving, students are open to confess needs that at other times remain locked in by timidity and fear. School problems, family discord, pressing temptations, grief, and discouragement often surface during a time of prayer at the altar. A teacher needs to be present to help a student find forgiveness and spiritual strength during these times of difficulty.

It is not easy to enumerate techniques for effective altar work, because the Spirit is sovereign, and it is His method that must be sought. However, several helpful observations can be made.

1. *Be courteous and polite.* Since the Spirit is gentle and forebearing, we who follow His leading should possess the same qualities. Some people are afraid to go to the altar because they imagine that someone will embarrass them by being discourteous and insensitive to their personal feelings.

2. *Be a good listener.* People in need are looking for a time

and place where they can express that need openly. Effective altar workers will listen intently and then pray specifically about a given area of concern. Many prayers are inappropriate because the counselor has failed to listen to what the person in need is saying.

3. *Follow through.* If a student is seeking to be filled with the Spirit, he should be encouraged to continue waiting on the Lord until that experience comes in fullness. If a student has a physical need and is prayed for at the altar, the teacher should be available later to encourage that student until the need is met. Some people who respond to an altar service will need to be directed to a Sunday school class or some other facet of the church's ministry.

Camping With a Goal

In recent years camping has opened up to the church a great opportunity for evangelism and ministry.

> A camp that changes life makes the most of its two greatest advantages: living in God's outdoor world, and living with counselor and cabinmates. It counteracts at least for a short period the church's discrepancy between knowing and doing. In our urbanized, depersonalized culture, young people crave the simplicity of going back to nature and elemental needs. Living like a pioneer becomes an adventure, not an inconvenience. Listening to frogs and woodpeckers and splashing waves relieves tension in nerves that are harassed by screeching traffic and fire sirens. An atmosphere in which God speaks through His second book of nature is conducive to hearing Him speak through His first Book of Scripture. The natural setting should be kept rustic, not civilized, with plenty of places for roaming and exploring.[2]

In increasing numbers, young people especially are responding to the atmosphere of camping, and in the camping experience finding Christ as Savior. A carefully developed camp program bridges the gap between theoretic and practical Christianity. Children see Christianity in practice on the ball field, at the lake, on hikes, and around the dinner table. Many adults in our churches look back to youth camp days as the time when they made important decisions about life and God. The church must use this great opportunity to evangelize the lost and lead believers to a place of spiritual maturity.

Whenever possible, Sunday school teachers should volunteer for counselor assignments in the church's camping program. If possible, a teacher should select that particular camp session when members of his own class will be present. Student interest will rise if they know that their teacher will be with them.

The camping program gives the teacher an opportunity to observe the students in a variety of experiences. Students who have been impossible to get next to may well open up in a camp setting. Students who have been loners come alive during the recreational periods at camp. And students who never seem to respond to an altar call in the home church are found seeking God in earnest at a vesper service. What a wonderful opportunity for teacher/student interaction!

Teachers, however, must prepare their students for post-camp reentry. "How come I get a better blessing at camp than at church?" This question points out a problem that can be very real. Young people and children find a security and release in the homogeneous atmosphere of a camp experience. To face life as it is back home for the other 51 weeks of the year calls for an adjustment. Wise leaders will bridge this gap by challenging the newly committed to carry the joy of their experience back to their home and church. The church must be prepared to capitalize on the zeal and excitement of returning campers.

Recreation and Re-creation

A concern for body, as well as mind and spirit, will open to the church many opportunities for evangelization. Children, youth, and even adults learn to relate to one another better through purposeful play activities. And out of true relationships is found the stuff that produces conversion experiences and spiritual growth. The love of Christ flows through but one channel—the yielded hearts of people. Many in our churches have come to Christ because of the warmth and compassion shown them through programs that serve both physical and spiritual needs.

Time and space do not permit a full explanation of all the opportunities for winning people to Christ beyond the classroom. What is included here is only meant to be suggestive.

The Spirit's Call

"How is a great church built?" "One person at a time!" How are persons brought into the kingdom of God and enfolded into the life and ministry of the church? One at a time. We are back to where we began, with the teacher using every possible means to win students to Jesus Christ and see them challenged and equipped to become a vital force in the work of the church. We dare not stop at anything less. This must be our goal and our focus, the motivating force of our devotion.

Church growth experts speak of looking at our world with "church growth eyes. That is, a mindset and a perspective that places the highest priority on winning the lost to Christ. This kind of focus sees in every situation the possibility of winning people to Christ. It is a view of the world that keeps asking, "How can we win people to Christ and bring them into the life and ministry of the church?"

When you read the daily newspaper, with its stories of relentless conflict, struggle, death, and war, do you see an opportunity to win the lost to Christ? When you look at your community in general and your neighbor in particular, do you see persons for whom Christ died? When you look at your own resources of giftedness, time, and money, do you see how enormous is your own capacity to influence people to come to Christ? When you evaluate the work of your own church, do you see the masses of people yet unreached by the gospel?

A pastor once made the shocking statement, "People are standing in line to receive Jesus Christ as Savior." I agree. It may not seem so. But if we have eyes for the lost we will see it as just that. People already under conviction, already prepared to hear, like ripe fruit waiting to be harvested. It is this spirit and attitude of heart that provides the motivational thrust to be a soul winner. Again, you are not alone. As a church fellowship we have committed ourselves to the task of world evangelization. In every church, section, district, region, and nation of the world the priority is the same—to win people to Jesus Christ and bring them into the fellowship of the church. "To every creature" is the order. The task is great, but so is our collective resolve.

Through the blessing and providence of God, an international network of indigenous churches, Bible training centers, printing presses, and media outreach facilities is in place around the world. Under the direction of Spirit-filled men and women, these agencies are coordinated to provide the means whereby our world can be reached for Jesus Christ. Never before in the history of the Christian Church has the opportunity for evangelism been greater. The Church now has at her disposal the means and methods whereby every creature can be reached with the gospel. The only unanswered question is one of resolve, dedication, and obedience.

You, the teacher, motivated by the love of Christ, empowered by the Holy Spirit, and moved to action by a heart of compassion, are the key player in the great task of winning the world to Christ. In your place, day by day, week by week, Sunday by Sunday, you offer to the lost a message of reconciliation, hope, peace, and fellowship. One by one you will win the lost to Christ and bring them into the life and ministry of the church.

In the brief time that remains, may every worker and teacher strive with renewed energy to touch as many lives as possible with the gospel of our Lord Jesus Christ. To this task the Spirit calls!

NOTES

[1] Larry Christenson, *The Christian Family* (Minneapolis, Minn.: Bethany Fellowship, 1970), 11–12.

[2] LeBar, *Focus on People in Church Education*, 194.

Bibliography

Caldwell, Irene S., Richard A. Hatch, and Beverly Welton. *Basics for Communication in the Church*. Anderson, Ind.: Warner Press, 1971.

Christenson, Larry. *The Christian Family*. Minneapolis, Minn.: Bethany Fellowship, 1970.

Coleman, Robert E. *The Master Plan of Evangelism*. Westwood, N.J.: Fleming H. Revell Company, 1963.

Dobbins, Gaines S. *Winning the Children*. Nashville, Tenn.: Broadway Press, 1953.

Edge, Findley B. *Helping the Teacher*. Nashville: Broadman Press, 1959.

_____. *Teaching for Results*. Nashville: Broadman Press, 1956.

Fulbright, Robert G. *New Dimensions in Teaching Children*. Nashville: Broadman Press, 1971.

Gangel, Kenneth O. *Leadership for Church Education*. Chicago: Moody Press, 1971.

Hakes, J. Edward, ed. *An Introduction to Evangelical Christian Education*. Chicago: Moody Press, 1971.

Hendricks, Howard. *Teaching To Change Lives*. Portland, Oreg.: Multnomah Press, 1987.

Hendricks, William. *A Theology for Children*. Nashville, Tenn.: Broadman Press, 1980.

Ingle, Clifford, ed. *Children and Conversion*. Nashville: Broadman Press, 1970.

Irving, Roy G. and Roy B. Zuck, eds. *Youth and the Church*. Chicago: Moody Press, 1968.

LeBar, Lois E. *Children in the Bible School*. Westwood, N.J.: Fleming H. Revell Company, 1958.

_____. *Focus on People in Christian Education*. Old Tappan, N.J.: Fleming H. Revell Company, 1968.

Martin, William J. *The Church in Mission.* Springfield, Mo.: Gospel Publishing House, 1986.

Richards, Lawrence O. *A Theology of Children's Ministry.* Grand Rapids, Mich.: Zondervan, 1983.

———. *Creative Bible Teaching.* Chicago: Moody Press, 1970.

Sapp, Phyllis Woodruff. *Creative Teaching in the Church School.* Nashville: Broadman Press, 1967.

Shelly, J.A. *The Spiritual Needs of Children.* Downers Grove, Ill.: InterVarsity Press, 1982.

Soderholm, Marjorie. *Explaining Salvation to Children.* Minneapolis, Minn.: Free Church Publications, 1962.

Taylor, Marvin J., ed. *An Introduction to Christian Education.* Nashville: Abingdon Press, 1966.

Westerhooff, John. *Will Our Children Have Faith.* Seabury, 1976.

Willis, Wesley. *Make Your Teaching Count.* Wheaton, Ill.: Scripture Press, 1985.

Zuck, Roy B., and Robert E. Clark, *Childhood Education in the Church.* Chicago: Moody Press, 1986.

Zuck, Roy B., and Gene A. Getz, eds. *Adult Education in the Church.* Chicago: Moody Press, 1970.